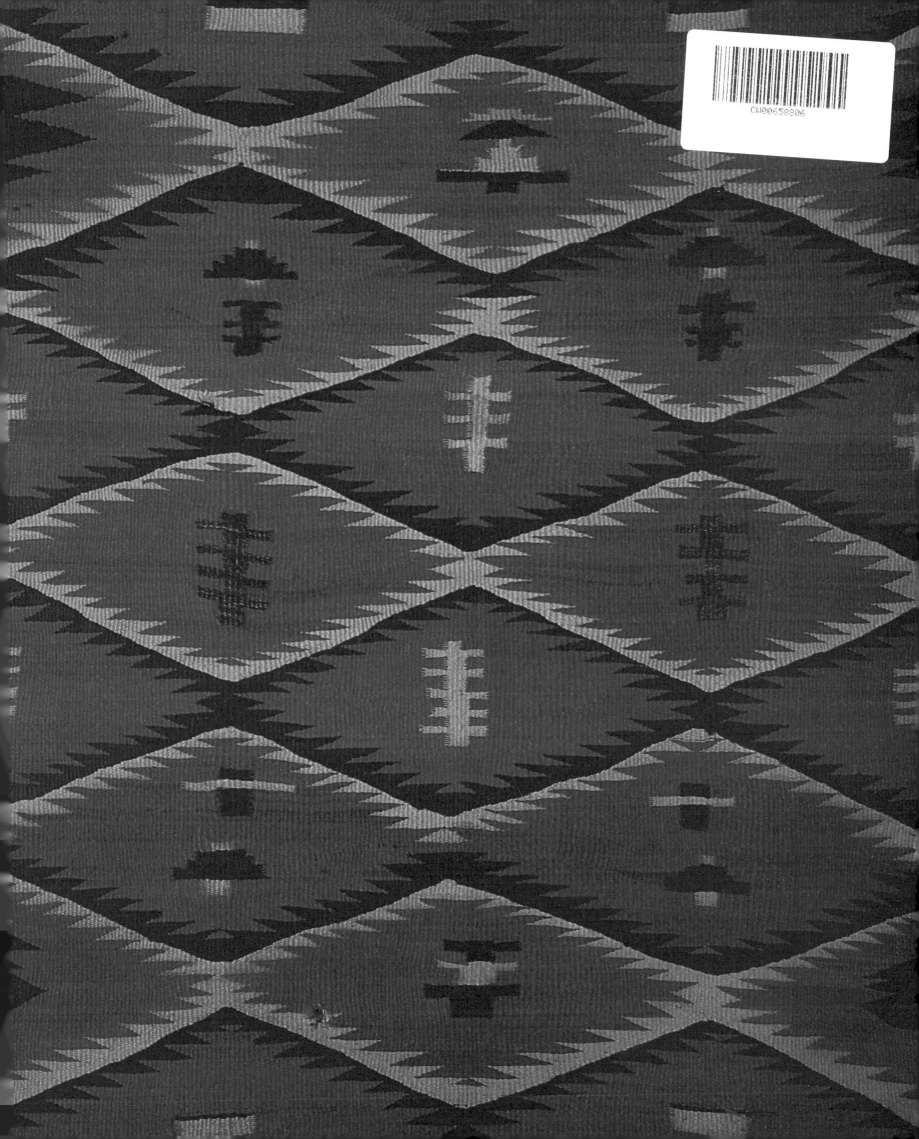

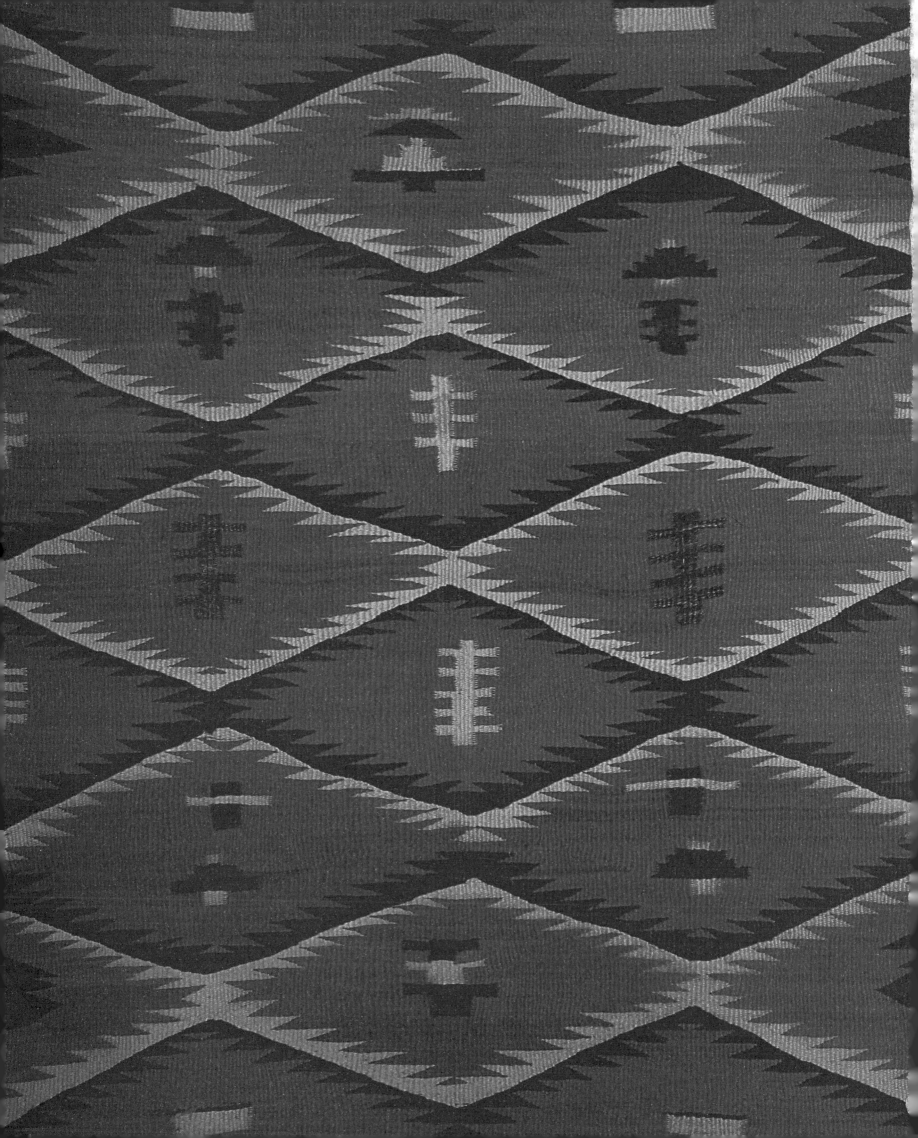

ARIZONA BILTMORE

JEWEL OF THE DESERT

History text by

JAMES A. CRUTCHFIELD

Photography by

ACKNOWLEDGMENTS

The publisher wishes to thank all of the individuals and organizations that graciously contributed time and expertise for the creation of this book. In particular, the greatest measure of gratitude is extended to Michael McMahon, Director of Sales and Marketing, for his original vision and enthusiastic support to bring the book to fruition.

Appreciation is also extended to Marketing Department staff members Stefanie Punch, Sarah Moran, Andra Dan, and Amina Ziri for their dedicated assistance in scheduling events and subjects portrayed in the book. Thank you to Randy Powers for his creative location scouting and assistance with culinary photography.

A special thanks goes to concierge and history tour director Kerwin Christian for providing valuable historical resources and information, and to hotel maître d' Geoffrey Weiss for his matchless arrangement in providing props and assistance. We are indebted to former Arizona Biltmore historian Becky Blaine for sharing her limitless knowledge of hotel history and lore.

We are grateful to Arizona State University archivist Harold Housley for providing archival photographs and information relating to the construction of the hotel, and to Albert Chase McArthur's son Manfred McArthur for providing personal family photographs of the architect.

Our appreciation is extended to the Frank Lloyd Wright Foundation at Taliesin West for photography related to Frank Lloyd Wright.

We also offer our gratitude to Executive Chef Gordon Maybury, Chef de Tournant Bryan Gorton, Wright's at the Biltmore manager Dolan Olson, and Frank and Albert's manager Tim Jesson for their guidance and assistance in portraying the culinary story of the hotel. Special thanks to photo shoot hair and make-up artist, Lana Khoury. Dick Bates, general manager of Arizona Biltmore Golf Club, was a gracious host in facilitating the photography of golf course scenery and activities.

Finally, no tribute to Arizona Biltmore would be complete without recognizing the warm friendliness of the doormen, wait staff, chefs, groundskeepers, and hospitality staff whose graciousness exemplifies the cornerstone of the Arizona Biltmore charm and tradition.

DUSK FROM THE ROOF TERRACE OF ARIZONA BILTMORE

PAGE 1: TWO OF THE FRANK LLOYD WRIGHT SPRITES WELCOME ARRIVING GUESTS AT THE
BILTMORE ESTATES DRIVE GATEWAY TO ARIZONA BILTMORE.
PREVIOUS SPREAD: THE ENCHANTING FRONT ENTRANCE TO ARIZONA BILTMORE

ARIZONA BILTMORE

JEWEL OF THE DESERT

It was quite a crowd that gathered near the foothills of what is now known as Piestewa Peak on Saturday, February 23, 1929, to participate in the three-day-long grand opening of the Arizona Biltmore Hotel. Located on several hundred acres of orange groves eight miles northeast of Phoenix amidst ancient irrigation canals built centuries earlier by members of the ancient Hohokam culture, the hostelry was billed as Arizona's first resort and was already being called the "Jewel of the Desert." Six-hundred invitations were mailed out to prospective attendees. Hotel management estimated that about one-third of that number would be able to attend, which would have been ideal because 243 rooms were available; however, the response was so great that a decision was made to recreate the opening gala three days in a row to accommodate the 600 guests. Two hundred additional guests requested permission to attend, but they could not be accommodated.

Those assembled were in awe as a small aircraft flew over the several structures that made up the resort. Few knew that the vice-president of the Arizona Biltmore Corporation, James Woods, was a passenger in the airplane and that it was he who dropped a bouquet of roses upon the amazed and delighted guests. Wrapped inside the roses was a single "key" to "open" the hotel, but when the roses landed on the roof, the ceremonies had to be delayed until the key could be retrieved and delivered to Charles Hervey, the hotel's general manager.

It was an affair unlike any that had ever been experienced by the residents of Phoenix and one that lived on in the memories of all who attended. As the hotel opened its doors to the gala crowd that bright Saturday in February, no one present could have imagined that almost eight months to the day later, Wall Street would crash, plunging the United States into the worst economic depression in its history.

THE PROGRAM AND MENU FOR OPENING WEEK CEREMONIES AT THE HOTEL

ABOVE AND LEFT: DURING THE ARIZONA-BILTMORE'S DEDICATION CEREMONIES, THIS LARGE WOODEN KEY, NESTLED IN A BOUQUET OF ROSES, WAS DROPPED FROM A SMALL AIRCRAFT AND USED TO SYMBOLICALLY "OPEN" THE HOTEL.

The Arizona Biltmore Hotel was the brainchild of two Phoenix residents, brothers Charles and Warren McArthur, who were the owners of a large Dodge automobile dealership as well as the first radio station in town, KFAD, which went on the air in 1922. The McArthurs were entrepreneurs to the

THE MCARTHUR BROTHERS CONVERTED DODGE TRUCKS INTO FORERUNNERS OF EARLY RVS, THE USE OF WHICH BY SIGHTSEERS STIMULATED EARLY TOURISM IN ARIZONA.

core, and as early as 1917 they had envisioned the construction of a tourist hotel near Phoenix. By the mid-1920s, the brothers' interest in the proposed hotel reached a fever pitch. A booming tourist industry had evolved in the region. Every passing year brought more health-seekers and sightseers to marvel at the majesty and wonder of America's great Southwest. The McArthurs had already experimented with a 1920s version of the present-day RV when they converted several Dodge trucks into "Wonderbuses," complete with bunk beds, expanded seating, a kitchen, and a bath with a shower. These improvised tour buses fit the bill for providing the growing number of visitors with the comfort and convenience they demanded.

By the mid-1920s, the population of Phoenix had reached nearly 37,000, having more than doubled in the dozen years since Arizona had

WARREN AND CHARLES MCARTHUR, OWNERS OF THE LARGEST DODGE AUTO DEALERSHIP IN ARIZONA, WERE AMONG THE PRIMARY ORGANIZERS OF THE ARIZONA-BILTMORE CORPORATION.

become the nation's forty-eighth state in 1912. With the encouraging population growth and the continuing expansion of the tourist industry, the McArthur brothers set their sights on other financially attractive opportunities. They visualized nothing but good times for Arizona in general and Phoenix in particular. What additional investment strategy could be more rewarding than the establishment of a grand hotel resort, aligned with arguably the most prestigious hospitality chain in the United States?

Looking for a sounding board and potential support for their idea, the brothers contacted John McEntee Bowman, a legend among American hoteliers, and the owner of the Biltmore chain of hotels with facilities in 14 cities, including Havana, Atlanta, New York City, and Los Angeles. Bowman was receptive to the idea

and the three embarked on a one million dollar fund-raising campaign for what they believed would be the Valley of the Sun's premier hotel. An early investor of the project was Chicago business mogul, William Wrigley Jr., owner of the Chicago Cubs baseball team and the Wrigley chewing gum empire. Wrigley Jr. offered an initial investment of $50,000. Additionally, a third McArthur brother, Albert Chase McArthur, an architect who early in his career had served as an apprentice draftsman

A MCARTHUR "WONDERBUS," ACCOMPANIED BY A "CHUCK" VEHICLE LOADED WITH FOOD AND SUPPLIES AND ATTENDED BY A PRIVATE CHEF

THE ARCHITECTURAL RECORD

ARIZONA BILTMORE HOTEL PHOENIX ARIZONA

"THE ARIZONA
BILTMORE
IS AN OFFSPRING
OF THE DESERT
AND IF I HAVE PLAYED
THE MIDWIFE
IN BRINGING
THIS CHILD
INTO THE WORLD,
I AM CONTENT."
—ALBERT CHASE MCARTHUR

ALTHOUGH ALBERT CHASE
MCARTHUR WAS THE ARCHITECT
OF RECORD FOR THE ARIZONA
BILTMORE HOTEL, HIS DESIGN
WAS HEAVILY INFLUENCED BY THE
EARLY WORK OF HIS MENTOR,
FRANK LLOYD WRIGHT.

to famed architect Frank Lloyd Wright and who had consulted with and provided ideas to his two brothers in 1917, was encouraged to revisit his earlier ideas about the hotel and to provide a workable design.

As Albert Chase McArthur delved into the planning of the proposed 243-room hotel, he decided that he wanted to use a particular kind of concrete block with a textured look as the primary building element. He knew that Frank Lloyd Wright had utilized these blocks in several of his California projects and assumed that Wright

owned the patent for the design. McArthur contacted Wright and offered him $10,000 for permission to use the blocks, a deal that Wright quickly accepted. At the time, Wright's business was apparently suffering from a lack of clientele, so he also offered his services to McArthur as a consultant. When the deal was done, McArthur had agreed to pay the master architect not only the $10,000 for use of what he thought was a

AN EARLY RENDERING OF ALBERT CHASE
MCARTHUR'S DESIGN FOR THE FRONT
ELEVATION OF THE ARIZONA BILTMORE

ALBERT CHASE McARTHUR
ENTRANCE AND FORECOURT

· ARCHITECT · · PHOENIX ·
ARIZONA BILTMORE · PHOENIX

patented concept, but also $1,000 per month for consulting fees. As it turned out, Wright did not own the patent to the block's design, a fact which when learned by McArthur, permanently soured the relationship between the two men.

The facility for the manufacture of the blocks was located on-site, using the surrounding desert sand for material and area workers for labor in order to reflect Frank Lloyd Wright's philosophy on using what nature provides. Although localized, the process was still a costly one. Noted sculptor Emry Kopta was commissioned to sculpt the molds for the blocks, the design of which his widow described as "based on the criss-crossed pattern of freshly trimmed trunks of palm trees," but which, according to writings of McArthur, were drawn by himself and "copied by a sculptor and adapted by him to the various other forms." The mini-factory turned out more than 250,000 blocks, which eventually found their way into the hotel's exterior and interior design. McArthur's plans also specified for the roof over the entire hotel to be fabricated from copper, a metal common in Arizona, but nonetheless expensive. Flower gardens, riding trails, a stable, a golf course, custom-designed furniture, a gym, a first-class restaurant, and original art were all elements that McArthur incorporated into his design.

The original investment of one million dollars was soon exhausted, leaving much to be done. A second investment of over one million dollars was then quickly disbursed, demanding the raising of still more cash. Mr. Wrigley was persuaded to eventually invest close to two million dollars , which made him the majority shareholder of the hotel and its properties. When the stock market fell in late October 1929, Wrigley was one of the few investors not so financially stressed that he had to dispose of his holdings.

LEFT: CONSTRUCTION OF THE LOBBY
BELOW: THE AZTEC ROOM AND MAIN BUILDING UNDER CONSTRUCTION

Arizona Biltmore 11-17-1928 #156

FROM AUGUST, 1928 UNTIL FEBRUARY, 1929, ONLY SIX MONTHS WERE REQUIRED TO BUILD THE ARIZONA BILTMORE. CONSTRUCTION CREWS WORKED AROUND THE CLOCK TO INSURE THAT THE GRAND OPENING CELEBRATION WOULD BE HELD ON TIME.

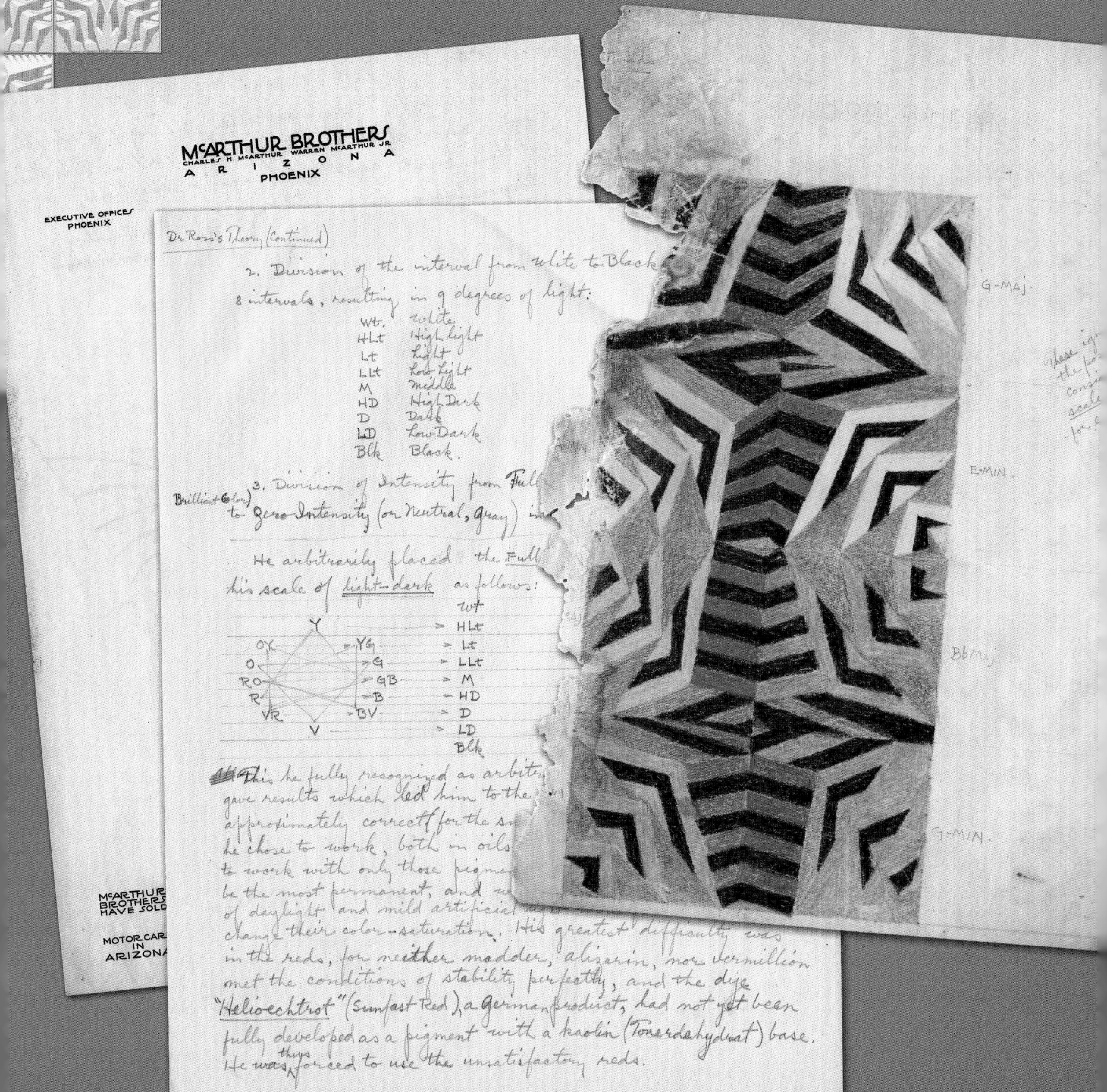

McARTHUR BROTHERS
CHARLES H. McARTHUR WARREN McARTHUR JR.
A R I Z O N A
PHOENIX

EXECUTIVE OFFICES
PHOENIX

McARTHUR
BROTHERS
HAVE SOLD

MOTOR CARS
IN
ARIZONA

Dr. Ross's Theory (Continued)

2. Division of the interval from White to Black
8 intervals, resulting in 9 degrees of light:

Wt.	White
HLt	High Light
Lt	Light
LLt	Low Light
M	Middle
HD	High Dark
D	Dark
LD	Low Dark
Blk	Black.

3. Division of Intensity from Full
Brilliant Color to Zero Intensity (or Neutral, Gray) in

He arbitrarily placed the Full
his scale of light—dark as follows:

This he fully recognized as arbit...
gave results which led him to the ...
approximately correct for the su...
he chose to work, both in oils ...
to work with only those pigme...
be the most permanent, and ...
of daylight and mild artificial ...
change their color—saturation. His greatest difficulty was
in the reds, for neither madder, alizarin, nor vermillion
met the conditions of stability perfectly, and the dye
"Helioechtrot" (Sunfast Red), a German product, had not yet been
fully developed as a pigment with a kaolin (Toxerdehydrat) base.
He was thus forced to use the unsatisfactory reds.

G-MAJ.

E-MIN.

Bb MAJ

G-MIN.

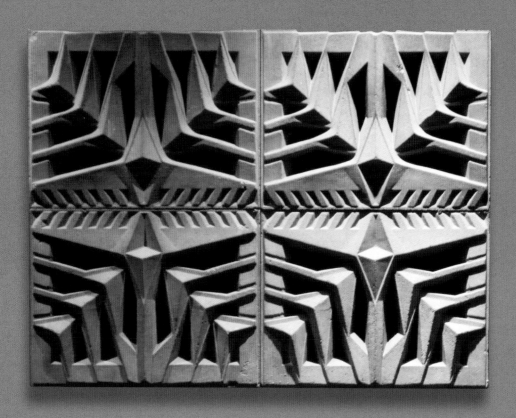

THE UNIQUE BILTMORE BLOCKS

If one could identify the single-most striking architectural feature of the Arizona Biltmore's design, it would no doubt be the "Biltmore Block." Albert Chase McArthur used 250,000 blocks, all manufactured on-site, in both the interior and exterior elements of the hotel. The blocks were designed by McArthur and sculpted by Emry Kopta. They were made of molded concrete, and each measured 18 inches long by 13 ½ inches high and from 3 ½ to 4 ½ inches thick. The blocks had grooved edges and when they were joined, the grooves were filled with cement grout and reinforced with steel rods, both horizontally and vertically. Two sheets of blocks were utilized in the hotel buildings' walls and the space between the sheets was reinforced with concrete. Interestingly, none of the dimensions on McArthur's plans, drawings, or blueprints had any reference to feet and inches. All measurements were noted in "units," a unit being defined as "the length of 6 horizontal cement blocks or 8 vertical blocks."

McArthur tinkered with many designs for the exposed face of the blocks and eventually settled on twenty-nine separate renderings, most of them used in the hotel, but a few not utilized at all.

During a magical evening in the desert outside Phoenix, formally attired guests arrived to the pomp and gaiety of an orchestra and the celebration heralding the premier opening night of Arizona Biltmore. It was during this February 23, 1929 evening to remember that the enduring metaphor "Jewel of the Desert" was first coined.

THE COMPLETED AZTEC ROOM
AND MAIN BUILDING

FRANK LLOYD WRIGHT AND ALBERT CHASE MCARTHUR

Although Albert Chase McArthur was the architect on record for the Arizona Biltmore Hotel, his mentor, the legendary Frank Lloyd Wright, has always been associated with the facility's construction. A connection between the two men did in fact exist during the project's early days. Wright came onboard when McArthur requested permission to utilize a type of "textile-block-slab construction" technique, invented by Wright several years earlier and used by him in some of his earlier designs. The request was complicated by McArthur's mistaken illusion that Wright owned the patent to the technique. Once the two men were onsite and McArthur learned that Wright did not own the patent—despite the fact that Wright had already accepted a $10,000 use fee from McArthur—the once-close personal relationship soon eroded, and Wright permanently left the project after participating in it for about five months.

Years later, McArthur wrote that between his early days as Wright's student and the time he contacted Wright about the use of the block design, the two men had communicated very

little, and during the interval, McArthur had developed "ideas which were at variance with his [Wright's], especially in regard to details," which would have made it "impossible for me to accept blindly all of his suggestions, as he would have liked to have had me do." Furthermore, McArthur revealed that when he and Wright parted ways, although the hotel plans were complete, later suggestions by engineers and others required that the plans be totally redone. He added, "Everything was revamped and redrawn [and] none of these final drawings was ever seen by Mr. Wright. All were made under my personal direction."

Wright eventually admitted that the design of the Arizona Biltmore was from the pen of Albert Chase McArthur alone and that he himself had little input into the project. In a letter addressed "To Whom it May Concern" and dated June 2, 1930, he wrote:

> All I have done in connection with the building of the Arizona Biltmore, near Phoenix, I have done for Albert McArthur himself at his sole request, and for none other. Albert McArthur is the architect of that building—all attempts to take the credit for that performance from him are gratuitous and beside the mark. But for him Phoenix would have had nothing like the Biltmore, and it is my hope that he may be enabled to give Phoenix many more beautiful buildings, as I believe him entirely capable of doing so.

As scores of civic and business leaders, invited guests, and other dignitaries filed into the Arizona Biltmore during the grand opening in late February 1929, they were profoundly impressed by the architectural majesty of the place. The book *Jewel of the Desert*, published in 2009 to celebrate the hotel's 80th anniversary, described the wondrous beauty that visitors beheld as they entered the fabulously decorated facility.

WESTERN ARTIST
MAYNARD DIXON

The main lobby and building are unequaled in both design and aesthetic beauty. Selected materials and design choices were all chosen to uphold the charm of a unique Western resort and this can all be found in the details, including everything from lighting choices to block patterns. The lighting was incorporated in the design through molded semi-opaque glass blocks inset to match the walls and supporting pillars of the lobby. Wrought iron pieces, from dining room lamps, andirons and ashtrays were custom manufactured to order, following patterns created by Warren and Albert McArthur, who also designed the furniture for all but one room of the resort. The only room that they did not design furniture for was the men's smoking room which was designed by Kem Weber, an interior designer brought in from Los Angeles.

Around the hotel complex, guests and visitors also found 15 individually designed cottages, which some sources maintain had a more direct Frank Lloyd Wright influence than other parts of the hotel. In addition, a magnificent mural measuring 25 feet by 8 feet, entitled "Legend of Earth and Sun" and painted by the noted Western artist Maynard Dixon, was hung from the ceiling of the Sun Room.

THE BILTMORE COTTAGES

MAYNARD DIXON PAINTED THE MURAL, "LEGEND OF EARTH AND SUN," (OPPOSITE PAGE) FOR THE ARIZONA BILTMORE'S GRAND OPENING AND YEARS LATER, HIS WIDOW, EDITH HAMLIN, COMPLETED A COMPANION PIECE, "TURQUOISE GODDESS AND WARRIOR TWINS" (BELOW).

THESE TWO PHOTOS DEPICT THE HOTEL'S MAGNIFICENT LOBBY SHORTLY AFTER THE GRAND OPENING.

THIS NEW YEAR'S DAY 1930 DINNER MENU PRESENTS A SAMPLING OF THE TASTY DISHES OFFERED IN THE HOTEL'S DINING FACILITIES.

The attendees had very little time to visit and give their stamp of approval on the Arizona Biltmore. Like most other pre–air conditioned hotels and resorts in the region that suspended operations for the summer, it would close its doors in just six weeks, and would reopen for its second season the following November, just a little over two weeks after Wall Street failed.

"Happy New Year"
Arizona Biltmore

JAN. 1

Dinner

Fruit Cup, Arizona

Clear Green Sea Turtle en Tasse

Ripe Olives

Fairy Toast

Celery en Branche

Dinner Rolls

Queen Olives

Walnut Bread

Amandes Salees

Casserolette of Fresh Lobster and Crab, Newburg

Breast of Chicken, Virginia Ham
with Fresh Mushrooms

New Garden Peas

Butter Ball Potatoes

Spiced Peaches

Punch Parfait, D'Amour

Salade Mylady
French, Roquefort or Epicurean Dressing

Frozen Egg Nogg

Nesselrode Pudding

Petit Fours

Roquefort or American Cheese
Toasted Bents or Saltine Wafers

Cafe Noir

After Din

DURING THE EARLY
DAYS OF OPERATION,
THE ARIZONA BILTMORE
EMPHASIZED THE "OLD
WEST" EXPERIENCE IN ITS
HOUSE BAND.

Despite the fact that the arrival of the Depression had placed a damper on many Phoenicians' social lives, the hotel's second opening outdid the first. Five hundred guests danced to the music of Harry Owens and the Arizona Biltmore Orchestra. Owens would go on to write the hit song, "Sweet Leilani," which earned him an Oscar in 1938 for Best Original Song and gave Bing Crosby his first gold record. The extravagant night proved to be a precursor of the atmosphere of magnificence and ebullience that the Arizona Biltmore would regularly provide for future visitors and guests.

Although the 1930s proved to be glorious years for the hotel and its guests, the decade started out in turmoil. By the time the business entered its second season, it became apparent to all that it could not continue to operate with the financial situation in which it found itself. Since Mr. Wrigley was by far the largest investor, he systematically acquired all of the shares of the Arizona Biltmore Corporation, the hotel's holding company, which he then dissolved. The McArthur brothers faded from the scene as well. Now entirely out of the Arizona Biltmore story, Charles and Warren returned east to New York City, and Albert moved to Los Angeles. Wrigley then restructured the hotel's management and set about enhancing its amenities by building the Catalina Pool, constructed with colorful clay tiles made on his Catalina Island property, and its associated bath

WILLIAM WRIGLEY JR.

house and cabanas. The Cowboy Bunk House, with stables to accommodate 80 horses, was opened to guests, giving an Old West look to the property. He appointed Bob Hunsick Jr., a future inductee into the Arizona Golf Hall of Fame, as pro for the hotel's Adobe golf course. He made provisions for extensive landscaping, road improvement, and the construction of three employee dormitories. And, in a stroke of genius, he hired Harry Boyle, a man who would become legendary as resident manager, to run the hotel's daily operations.

THE ORIGINAL ADOBE GOLF COURSE CLUB HOUSE

THE COWBOY BUNK HOUSE AND ITS CORRAL OF 80 HORSES PROVIDED SOME GUESTS WITH THEIR FIRST GLIMPSE OF WESTERN LIFE IN THE OLD DAYS.

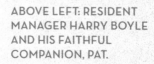

Wrigley became so enamored with the Phoenix area that he even decided to build a winter home there for himself and his family. Named "La Colina Solana," the 24-room structure dominated a hilltop just southwest of the hotel, overlooking Phoenix. He also began developing surrounding properties into home sites, the genesis of the present-day Biltmore Estates. With all of these hotel improvement plans and residential building possibilities whirling around in his mind, William Wrigley Jr. died on January 26, 1932, without ever having realized many of his dreams.

Harry Boyle, the new resident manager, became a permanent fixture in the hotel, keeping an eye on each and every detail that might enhance a guest's experience. With his dog, Pat, he could be seen at practically any time of the day and late into the night, pampering diners and tourists as they roamed the vast lobby. Boyle ran a tight ship, especially when it came to dining. Formal dress was not only required in the lobby after 6:00 p.m. but it was also a requisite for dinner, which was always served in the magnificent Gold Room promptly at 6:00 p.m., with no exceptions. On many occasions, guests were turned away from dinner when the magic hour arrived and they had not announced themselves on time. Boyle simply closed the curtains on the Gold Room doors to the lobby and refused to allow anyone else to enter.

ABOVE LEFT: RESIDENT MANAGER HARRY BOYLE AND HIS FAITHFUL COMPANION, PAT.

ABOVE: HARRY BOYLE AND GOLF PRO BOB HUNSICK JR.

WILLIAM WRIGLEY'S PHOENIX HOME, LA COLINA SOLANA

of P. K. Wrigley, Biltmore Estates, Phoenix, Arizona

6A-H710

MRS. WRIGLEY'S HILLTOP MANSION

Soon after becoming involved in the early phases of financing the Arizona Biltmore Hotel, William Wrigley Jr., the son of a soap manufacturer, decided to build a winter home atop a knoll overlooking the hostelry's premises. As a young man, Wrigley had moved from his native Philadelphia to Chicago and organized the William Wrigley Jr. Company, a manufacturer and purveyor of Wrigley's Scouring Soap. The young entrepreneur soon began offering premiums with his soap—first baking powder and later chewing gum—and when the chewing gum's popularity overpowered that of the soap, he introduced to the world Wrigley's Spearmint and Juicy Fruit chewing gums. By 1919, Wrigley had reached the status of multi-millionaire and purchased Catalina Island off the coast of Los Angeles.

In 1931, his 24-room home (with 17 bathrooms) was completed and presented to his wife, Ada, as a present. Eleven fireplaces, original artwork, a gold-leaf ceiling in the Rotunda, and formal living and dining rooms created by Italian craftsmen all blended into making the Wrigley Mansion one of the most magnificent homes in Arizona. The mansion, although today under different ownership from the hotel, offers guided tours of the premises, which gives the visitor an insight into the personal life and genius of the man who rescued the Arizona Biltmore Hotel from the depths of the Depression.

THE CATALINA POOL

William Wrigley once declared, "When two men in business always agree, one of them is unnecessary." Following this enterprising principle, the chewing gum empire mogul and baseball club owner correctly predicted the glowing future of Catalina Island, located off the coast of southern California, when, in 1919, he purchased the 112,000-acre island and turned it into a first-class vacation destination.

Over time, Wrigley oversaw the construction of 2,500 "bungalettes" each one accommodating two to three guests. Tropical gardens, aviaries, swimming, surfing, and the excitement of watching the Chicago Cubs in spring training were just a few of the attractions that awaited the tourist. Paying homage to his California days, Wrigley used tiles manufactured on Catalina Island to build the Catalina Pool at the Arizona Biltmore. The dazzling pool was often frequented by noted show business personality guests, such as Marilyn Monroe and Irving Berlin.

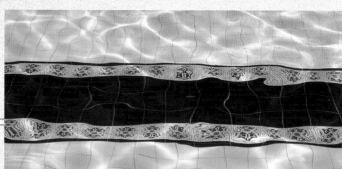

The Aztec Room, with its copper beams and gold-gilded ceiling, was a popular meeting place during the hotel's early years. Before television, the Wrigley's used it as a movie screening room and for parties. Other pastimes of the era included hayrides, horseback riding, and visits to the nearby replications of Mexican and Apache

AFTER CHECKING THE LATEST STOCK PRICES ON THE ARIZONA BILTMORE'S "BIG BOARD," A GUEST COULD WALK DOWN THE HALL AND ENJOY A LEISURELY GAME OF BILLIARDS.

MASTER BARTENDER GENE SULIT

Indian villages, which were built to give the curious tourist crowd a feel of how life was lived in the great Southwest in bygone days. From the late 1930s on, guests could also enjoy a fabulous drink, the Tequila Sunrise, invented by the hotel's own bartender, Gene Sulit.

THE HOTEL'S SEVERAL BALLROOMS PROVIDED AMPLE SPACE FOR JUST ABOUT ANY TYPE OF EVENT, WHETHER IT BE A FORMAL DINNER OR A DANCE.

During the 43 years of Wrigley family stewardship, the facility was operated as a kind of "hotel for the rich and famous." Although guests paid for their lodging and food, they could experience the Arizona Biltmore's finery only by personal invitation from the Wrigley family. In the very early days, the room rate was $20 per day for the American plan (no meals included in the rate) or $30 per day for the European plan (which included meals). With rates as low as they were over the years, the hotel made very little profit, which was one of the reasons the Wrigley family disposed of the property in 1973. Many guests stayed the entire season (from November until May) and returned year after year. Hopeful future guests knew they were invited when they received a locked invitation, to be followed up later with the key that unlocked it. The story goes that if children accompanied their parents, they spent most of their time being cared for in the cottages by their nannies, thereby not disturbing other guests.

DUE WARNING. Here's the ke... that fits the lock. You use it en... tirely at your own risk of finding yourself possessed with the desire to forsake all other plans and places for a winter at Arizona Biltmore !!!

ARIZONA BILTMORE
IN THE DESERT NEAR PHOENIX, U.S.A.

THE

ARIZONA
BILTMORE

Open from
November to May

On the Desert—near Phoenix

Write to Harry Boyle, Manager

DURING PROHIBITION, THE MEN'S "SMOKER" ROOM WAS CONVERTED INTO A SPEAKEASY (NOW CALLED THE MYSTERY ROOM) WHERE GUESTS COULD SAFELY INDULGE IN ALCOHOL.

When Prohibition reigned across the nation, the management of most esteemed hotels discovered ways to elude local law enforcement from bothering the guests who appreciated a libation or two while on vacation. At the Arizona Biltmore, a room that had originally been utilized as a men's smoker room was converted into a sort of "speak-easy" to which guests could retreat and be served alcoholic beverages. Called the Mystery Room, it was outfitted with a liquor cabinet that converted to a bookcase if a police raid occurred. The single skylight in the Mystery Room's ceiling was constantly being observed by a watchman on the alert for flashing lights blazing across the desert sky which a watchful employee would flash if and when the law did approach.

During the 1930s through the 1960s, the hotel played host to a myriad of Hollywood and show business luminaries, U. S. presidents, and sports notables, as well as public figures and those who wanted to be public figures. Silver-screen idols Clark Gable and Carole Lombard spent their honeymoon at the hotel, as well as future American President and First Lady Ronald and Nancy Reagan. One day while playing golf, Gable lost his brand-new wedding ring, and breathed a sigh of relief when an alert employee recovered it. Irving Berlin is said to have written his opus, "White Christmas," during one of his frequent visits. Marilyn Monroe often relaxed by the Catalina Pool.

Throughout the entire Wrigley ownership, the hotel had basically maintained its original look. No guest rooms had been added with the total remaining at 243. However, the buildings were air conditioned during 1963, requiring a helicopter to lower the units onto the roof since cranes were unable to position themselves properly to unload the heavy equipment. In 1969, the Grand Ballroom was opened, adding 6,500 square feet of meeting space.

PHOTOS TOP TO BOTTOM: SINGER AND ACTOR DEAN MARTIN (RIGHT), ACTOR RANDOLPH SCOTT (RIGHT) AND GOLF PRO BOB HUNSICK JR., COMEDIENNE MARTHA RAE, ACTOR CLARK GABLE (CENTER)

RONALD REAGAN
40TH PRESIDENT

WELCOME MISTER PRESIDENT

In early March, 1952, Miss Nancy Davis called Harry Boyle, the Arizona-Biltmore's general manager, and reserved accommodations for herself and her husband-to-be, actor Ronald Reagan. The Hollywood couple was married on March 5 and stayed at the hotel until March 13. Ronald Reagan was among several American presidents, some accompanied by their wives, to visit the "Jewel of the Desert." Others included Herbert Hoover, Harry Truman, Dwight D. Eisenhower, John F. Kennedy, Lyndon B. Johnson, Richard Nixon, Gerald Ford, Jimmy Carter, and George H. W. Bush.

HARRY S. TRUMAN
33RD PRESIDENT

JOHN F. KENNEDY
35TH PRESIDENT

DWIGHT D. EISENHOWER
34TH PRESIDENT

JIMMY CARTER
39TH PRESIDENT

RICHARD NIXON
37TH PRESIDENT

HERBERT HOOVER
31ST PRESIDENT

LYNDON B. JOHNSON
36TH PRESIDENT

GERALD FORD
38TH PRESIDENT

GEORGE H. W. BUSH
41ST PRESIDENT

As the years passed, the Wrigley family became less and less personally involved in the operation of the Arizona Biltmore and feelers were put out for a potential buyer. Mrs. Philip K. Wrigley, the daughter-in-law of William Wrigley Jr., revealed the reason for disposing of the property when she explained,

Now that we no longer come to Arizona or can personally supervise the hotel, we believe we should sell it. Yet, I could never part with this wonderful building unless I were absolutely assured that the new owners will cherish it as we have, of that you may be certain. We will only sell to someone who will take care of it and truly appreciate its remarkable beauty.

It was a sad time when the Wrigleys decided to sell the Arizona Biltmore in 1973, yet one that promised an even bigger and better future. Talley Industries, a Mesa, Arizona-based conglomerate that began operations in 1960 as a small aerospace engineering firm, but which had also discovered a profitable niche in real estate investment, became the hotel's new owner in 1973. Talley had plans for a major upgrade, but two weeks later, instead of the "Jewel of the Desert" embarking on an exciting new era, its entire fourth floor was destroyed by a disastrous six-alarm fire that also left significant smoke and water damage to the rest of the main building. According to one account, "The fire brought changes about more rapidly than planned," causing "everything [to be] discarded due to damage by fire, smoke, or water....The hotel had to be completely rebuilt, redecorated, and refurbished in ninety days," in time for a late September opening for the winter season. During 1928–29, from groundbreaking until completion, six months had been required to build the original structure. Many wondered if the same feat could be accomplished in only half that time.

FOLLOWING THE DISASTROUS FIRE OF 1973, THE ARIZONA BILTMORE SPRANG BACK TO LIFE IN RECORD TIME.

To call the monumental struggle to literally rebuild the Arizona Biltmore from scratch a Herculean effort would be a vast understatement. The smoke had hardly cleared from the ruins before block-making equipment was brought onto the property and commenced churning out the unique blocks that Albert Chase McArthur had utilized in the original edifice forty-five years earlier. Hotel management reached out to members of Taliesin Associated Architects, who were domiciled at the original Frank Lloyd Wright estate in Wisconsin. Many of these

FRANK LLOYD WRIGHT'S TALIESIN WEST

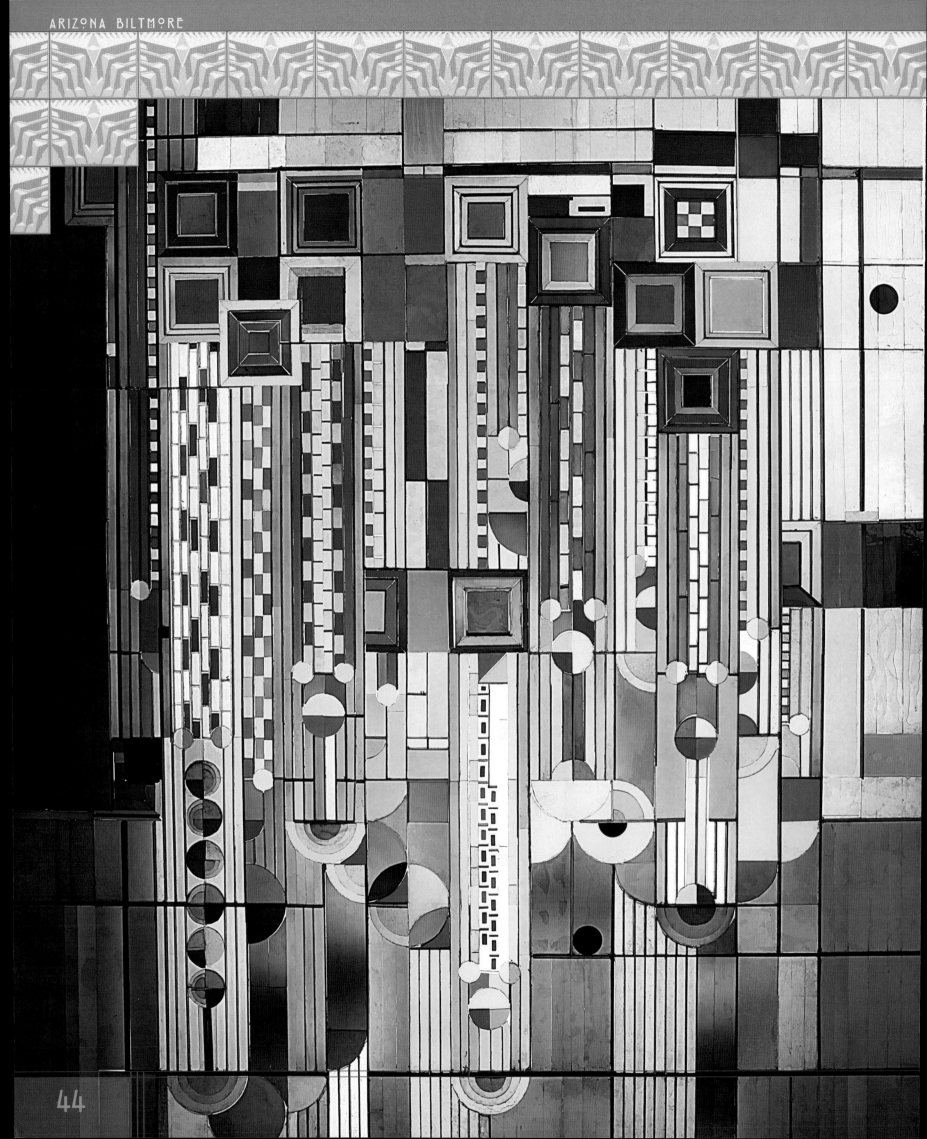

Wright disciples, as well as scores of craftsmen and workers from the Phoenix area, quickly volunteered their talents to the reconstruction of the hotel. The ceiling of the magnificent Gold Room was refurbished and is still maintained on record as the second largest gold-gilded feature in the world, next to the Taj Mahal. Maynard Dixon's widow, Edith Hamlin, traveled from California to refurbish not only Dixon's original mural, "Legend of Earth and Sun," but to renew her own "Turquoise Goddess and Warrior Twins,"

a companion piece that dated back to 1949. And Mrs. Olgivanna Wright gifted the hotel with a specially commissioned stained glass mural based on one of her late husband's colored pencil designs originally created in the late 1920s. The mural, "Saguaro Forms and Cactus Flowers," remains the centerpiece in the entrance as guests make their way to the registration desk.

Under the watchful eye of the new owner's wife, Mrs. Franz G. Talley, the Arizona Biltmore Hotel was reborn during the summer of 1973, and when the 1973–74 season opened on September 29, the reception was one of *déjà vu*. Adding to the glitz and glitter excitement of the grand reopening forty-four years after the first accepted guests checked in, the announcement was made that with the current season, the hotel would remain open for business year-around.

The first few years of Talley ownership were ones of expansion at the hotel. In 1975, the construction of the Paradise Wing added ninety state-of-the-art rooms, the first increase of the

OPPOSITE: "SAGUARO FORMS AND CACTUS FLOWER'S," THE IMPRESSIVE STAINED GLASS MURAL IN THE FRONT ENTRANCE, WAS ORIGINALLY SKETCHED IN COLORED PENCIL BY FRANK LLOYD WRIGHT, AND LATER COMMISSIONED IN GLASS BY WRIGHT'S WIDOW, OLGIVANNA AS A GIFT TO ARIZONA BILTMORE DURING THE 1973 RESTORATION.

THE PARADISE GARDEN (FAR LEFT) AND THE PARADISE WING

hotel's room count since the original opening in 1929. A second golf course, The Links, was opened in 1979 and its instant popularity, along with that of the original Adobe course, quickly earned the Arizona Biltmore a firm reputation as being *the* place in Phoenix to tee off. In 1979, the Valley Wing's completion provided 120 more rooms, in addition to the 39,000-square-foot Conference Center. In the meantime, by 1977,

the rapid growth of Phoenix had reached the vicinity of the hotel, and the Cowboy Bunkhouse and stables were razed to make room for new commercial development in the neighborhood.

The decade of the 1980s witnessed the completion of the 109-room Terrace Court Wing, a renovation of the lobby and 120 guest rooms in the main building, the opening of the East and Garden Wings, and the renovation of the cottages. A 22,000-square-foot spa, beauty salon, and fitness center were opened on the property in 1998, and the following year, a four-year, $50-million refurbishing and renovation of the facility was completed. The comprehensive project included the addition of The Villas luxury residential units, the opening of the Arizona Wing with 120 new guest rooms, two additional meeting rooms, and an Olympic-sized swimming pool. Total rooms in the hotel reached an all-time high of 740.

THE ADOBE GOLF COURSE (ABOVE) DATES BACK TO THE ORIGINAL OPENING OF THE ARIZONA BILTMORE. A SECOND COURSE, THE LINKS (BELOW), WAS DEDICATED IN 1979.

GARDEN WING AND PARADISE GARDENS

During 2000, the Arizona Biltmore was sold to KSL Recreation Corporation, a premier California hospitality concern which owned several world-class hotels, spas, and golf resorts. In 2002, KSL management oversaw a $60 million expansion that included the opening of the McArthur Ballroom with 15,000 square feet of dining and meeting space, as well as upgrades to guest rooms and the lobby. The last major projects performed by the KSL ownership were the 2003 completion of the Frank Lloyd Wright Ballroom, which increased the hotel's total meeting space to 100,000 square feet, and the $4 million renovation and upgrade of the Adobe golf course the following year.

THE LUXURIOUS GROUNDS AND GARDENS AT THE ARIZONA BILTMORE PROVIDE A WELCOME RESPITE TO THE HEAT OF THE SURROUNDING DESERT FOR MANY OF OUR INDIGENOUS RESIDENTS.

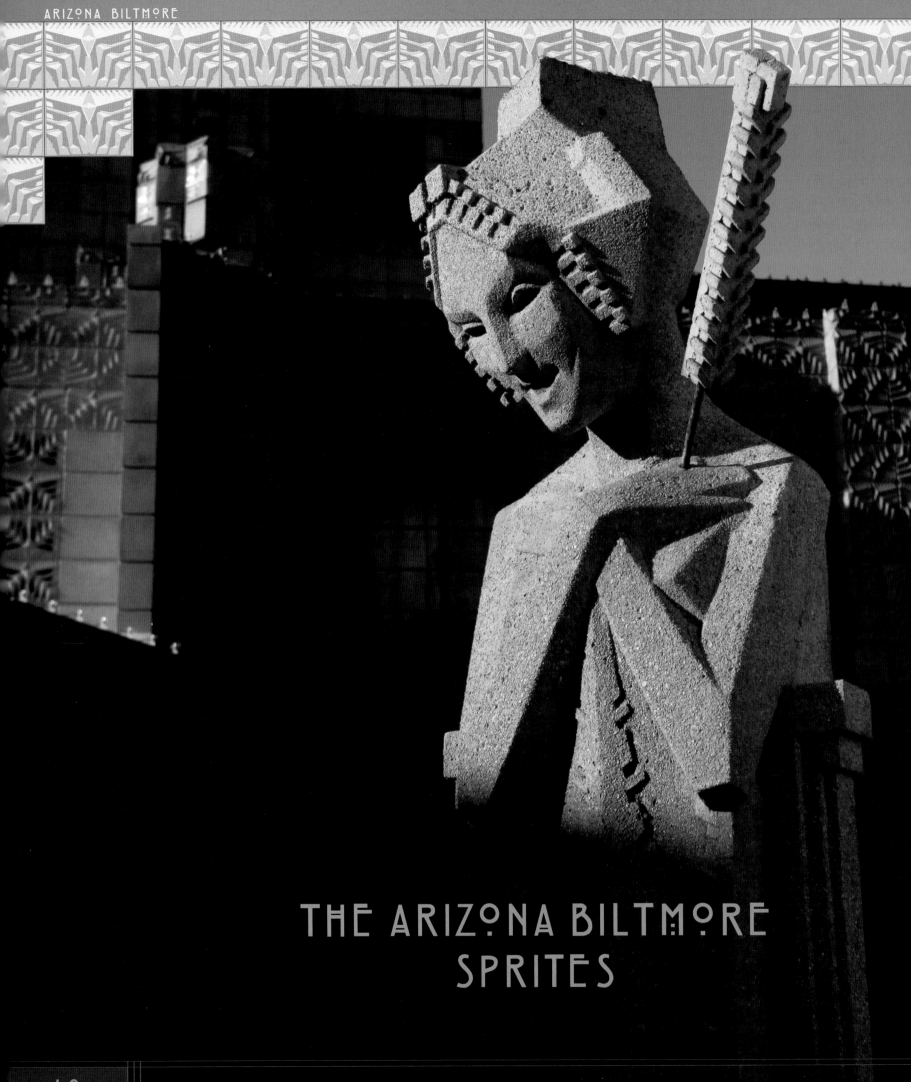

THE ARIZONA BILTMORE
SPRITES

As war clouds over Europe brought the Great World War into reality, residents of Chicago sought relief from the tragedy overseas by regularly visiting the Midway Gardens. Envisioned and created on the shores of Lake Michigan in 1914, the gardens were designed by Frank Lloyd Wright to provide a huge restaurant and entertainment center for locals and tourists alike. Wright, using his already famous "prairie style" of architecture, designed a complex reminiscent of an Oriental palace, complete with brilliant red roofs combined with both indoor and outdoor elements woven into a single whole. The use in the buildings of precast concrete panels, described by one authority as being designed in a "textile way," is reminiscent of the blocks used in the Arizona Biltmore.

One of the hallmarks of the Midway Gardens was a series of "sprites" designed by Wright and sculpted by Alfonso Iannelli. The heroic-sized figures were lost when the gardens were demolished in 1929, only to be rediscovered after World War II in a farmer's field in the Wisconsin Dells. Three of the statues were recovered by officials at Taliesin, Wright's original school in Wisconsin, and were sent to Mr. and Mrs. Don Lovness, who lived in a Frank Lloyd Wright–designed home in Stillwater, Minnesota. Mr. and Mrs. Lovness restored the sprites, which eventually made their way to Taliesin West, near Scottsdale, to become part of Mrs. Olgivanna Wright's newly created gardens. Replicas of the sprites were made, and six of them—each weighing 450 pounds and standing six feet tall—were donated by Taliesin in 1985 to the Arizona Biltmore. Today, these tributes to her husband watch over the Arizona Biltmore grounds.

RIGHT: PARADISE POOL

In 2007, the Arizona Biltmore joined the prestigious Waldorf Astoria Hotels and Resorts, an expanding portfolio of iconic luxury properties managed by Hilton Worldwide. Under Hilton's management, The Ocatilla at The Biltmore opened in 2009, the year of the hotel's 80th anniversary. The Ocatilla replaced the earlier Arizona Wing, which was totally redesigned and renovated. It is often referred to as "a hotel within the hotel," and provides luxury accommodations throughout its 120-room complex, including the private Ocatilla swimming pool, custom-furnished guest rooms and a private club inspired by Frank Lloyd Wright features, and private "in-complex" dining facilities.

The following year, the popular Biltmore Grill was replaced by Frank & Alberts, which features a variety of American comfort foods with a Sonoran flair. Whenever possible, the diverse menu offers meals made from organic ingredients acquired from local farmers and producers. During 2011, Wright's at The Biltmore, the hotel's signature restaurant, reopened following a major renovation

OPPOSITE: WRIGHT'S AT THE BILTMORE

BELOW: FRANK & ALBERT'S RESTAURANT

which included a new wine cellar that seats up to eight private diners. The revised wine list offers 470 unique labels and 3,700 bottles. Guest rooms in the Main Building and the East Wing were also completely renovated during 2011.

In March 2013, GIC Private Limited, the sovereign wealth fund of the Government of Singapore, purchased the Arizona Biltmore, A Waldorf Astoria Resort, along with the Grand Wailea, A Waldorf Astoria Resort in Maui, and La Quinta, A Waldorf Astoria Resort in the Palm Springs area. The property team and the new ownership group developed a capital improvement plan to restore the hotel to its original grandeur. The extensive, multi-million-dollar property renovation project was completed in fall of 2014. Included in the upgrades were re-mastering of guest rooms and suites, as well as meeting spaces, the Mystery Room, and ballrooms. The renovation included accommodations at the Garden, Valley, Paradise, and Terrace Court Wings, as well as those at the Cottages. The summer of 2013 witnessed the fifteen cabanas lining the Paradise Pool receiving upgrades, which included new interiors and HDTVs.

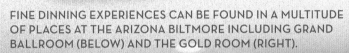

FINE DINNING EXPERIENCES CAN BE FOUND IN A MULTITUDE OF PLACES AT THE ARIZONA BILTMORE INCLUDING GRAND BALLROOM (BELOW) AND THE GOLD ROOM (RIGHT).

THE MAGNIFICENT CEILING OF ARIZONA BILTMORE'S GOLD ROOM IS THE SECOND LARGEST GOLD-GILDED FEATURE IN THE WORLD, NEXT TO THE TAJ MAHAL.

From the moment of its first opening in 1929, the internationally acclaimed Arizona Biltmore Hotel has been revered by all who visit. The resort instantly became one of America's most popular and luxurious destinations, drawing visitors from around the world to its exotic setting in the midst of Arizona's Sonoran Desert. Albert Chase McArthur, a brilliant yet relatively unknown architect, designed the many buildings scattered across the vast hotel property, and it is obvious that he was influenced by one of the period's foremost architects, his mentor, Frank Lloyd Wright.

Although McArthur and his two brothers, Warren and Charles, lost ownership of the hotel within a year after its grand opening, they were succeeded by William Wrigley Jr. and the Wrigley family, whose love of Phoenix, the desert, and the fabulous hotel they had acquired would leave an indelible stamp upon the property for many years to come.

After the great fire of 1973, the Wrigley family's successor, the Talley Corporation, engineered the Arizona Biltmore's rise from the ashes—much as the legendary Phoenix bird of ancient mythology arose and escaped from the flames—to reposition itself among the finest

hotels in the United States. KSL Recreation Corporation's acquisition of the Arizona Biltmore brought on a great expansion of ballroom space and golf facilities.

Over the years the previous owners have seen the Arizona Biltmore become the recipient of numerous national awards attesting to the hotel's place among the finest hostelries in North America and the world, among them, the AAA Four Diamond Award on multiple occasions; *Global Traveler*'s number five Best Hotel in the Western U. S.; the *Fodor's Travel Guides'* Choice Award for Best Places to Visit; one of *Travel and Leisure* magazine's Top 500 Hotels in the World; and an Award of Distinction from the Travel Channel's *Great Hotels Series*. The current operators and owners, the Waldorf Astoria Hotels & Resorts and GIC Private Limited, are equally committed to maintain the Arizona Biltmore's place as one of North America's finest and most renowned travel destinations and corporate meeting facilities.

BREAKFAST AT FRANK AND ALBERT'S

RIGHT: ROOM SERVICE IS DELIVERED WITH CHEERFUL APLOMB
PREVIOUS SPREAD: LUXURIOUS FRONT ENTRANCE GARDENS
PAGE 54-55: DAWN ON SQUAW PEAK TERRACE

CHEFS HARVEST ORANGES, LEMONS, AND CUMQUATS FROM TREES ON ARIZONA BILTMORE'S GROUNDS FOR USE IN VARIOUS CULINARY RECIPES.

PREVIOUS SPREAD: EARLY MORNING ON THE TERRACE OF A GARDEN COTTAGE
FOLLOWING SPREAD: MORNING SERENITY OF THE SPA EXPERIENCE

CLASSIC SOUTHWEST ARCHITECTURE IN HARMONY WITH A VERDANT, TROPICAL OASIS

PREVIOUS SPREAD: HOTEL MAÎTRE'D GEOFFREY WEISS AND THE FRONT LOBBY RECEPTION DESK
FOLLOWING SPREAD: ARRIVAL AT ARIZONA BILTMORE IS AN ENCHANTING EVENT FOR THE ENTIRE FAMILY.

BANQUET KITCHEN PREP LINE

RIGHT: EXECUTIVE CHEF GORDON MAYBURY APPLYING THE FINAL TOUCH TO BEEF WELLINGTON
PREVIOUS SPREAD: EXECUTIVE CHEF GORDON MAYBURY AND HIS TEAM OF SOUS CHEFS

SIGNATURE ENTRÉE AND DESSERT AT WRIGHT'S AT THE BILTMORE

BANQUET PASTERY CHEF

PREVIOUS SPREAD: BANQUET PREPARATIONS FOR THE GOLD BALLROOM

WOOD-FIRED OVEN ENTRÉES AT FRANK AND ALBERT'S

PASTRY CHEF LEOBARDO RAMIREZ

RIGHT: LEGENDARY TEA SOMMELIER KEVIN DOYLE SERVES AFTERNOON TEA IN THE LOBBY.
PREVIOUS SPREAD: TERRACE DINING AT FRANK AND ALBERT'S

PREPARING FOR A GALA EVENT IN THE MCARTHUR BALLROOM

FINAL PREPARATIONS IN THE FRANK LLOYD WRIGHT BALLROOM

FOLLOWING SPREAD: WRIGHT'S AT THE BILTMORE PRIVATE DINING ROOM

ENTRANCE TO THE ARIZONA BILTMORE

RIGHT: THE BREATHTAKING CEILING OF THE LEGENDARY AZTEC ROOM

EARLY MORNING ABOVE THE FOUNTAIN COURT GARDENS

RIGHT: WRIGHT'S AT THE BILTMORE PRIVATE DINING ROOM
PREVIOUS SPREAD: PARADISE GARDENS

BILTMORE CHAMPIONSHIP PUTTING COURSE AT COTTAGE COURT

THE FAMOUS #15 TEE OF ARIZONA BILTMORE'S LINKS GOLF COURSE WITH SQUAW PEAK IN THE BACKGROUND

EARLY MORNING AT PARADISE POOL

RIGHT: FAMILY FUN AT THE PARADISE POOL WATERSLIDE
PREVIOUS SPREAD: PUTTING PRACTICE ON SQUAW PEAK LAWN

WINNERS IN CLASS, CONCOURS D'ELEGANCE

RIGHT: CONCOURS D'ELEGANCE
PREVIOUS SPREAD: THE ANNUAL CONCOURS D'ELEGANCE GRACES THE ARIZONA BILTMORE LAWNS.

CONCOURS D'ELEGANCE

CONCOURS D'ELEGANCE

FOLLOWING SPREAD: CONCOURS D'ELEGANCE GRAND PRIZE WINNER AND EVENT HOSTESSES

ARIZONA BILTMORE IS A "PET FRIENDLY" RESORT.

RIGHT: THE GRACEFUL FRANK LLOYD WRIGHT SPRITES WELCOME GUESTS AND AVIAN FRIENDS AT THE FRONT ENTRANCE.
PREVIOUS SPREAD: AFTERNOON RELAXATION ON SQUAW PEAK LAWN

FORMAL EVENING EVENT IN THE MAIN LOBBY

RIGHT: ARIZONA BILTMORE IS ARIZONA'S MOST MEMORABLE WEDDING VENUE.
PREVIOUS SPREAD: WRIGHT'S AT THE BILTMORE MANAGER DOLAN OLSON STEWARDS THE EXTENSIVE WINE CELLAR.
FOLLOWING SPREAD: WINE AT DUSK ON SQUAW PEAK TERRACE

THE ARIZONA BILTMORE CHRISTMAS TREE

THE MAIN LOBBY AT CHRISTMAS SEASON
FOLLOWING SPREAD: CHRISTMAS IS A MAGICAL SEASON AT ARIZONA BILTMORE.

THE LEGENDARY "TEQUILA SUNRISE" WAS CREATED AT ARIZONA BILTMORE IN THE 1930S AND HAS NEVER WANED IN POPULARITY.

THE SUBTLE MYSTERY OF MOONLIGHT AND DESERT FRAGRANCE EMBRACES THE ARIZONA BILTMORE SPRITES AT DUSK.

SQUAW PEAK LAWN AT DUSK

RIGHT: ROASTING MARSHMALLOWS ON SQUAW PEAK TERRACE IS A FAMILY TRADITION.
FOLLOWING PAGE: THE GARDEN OASIS OF PARADISE POOL

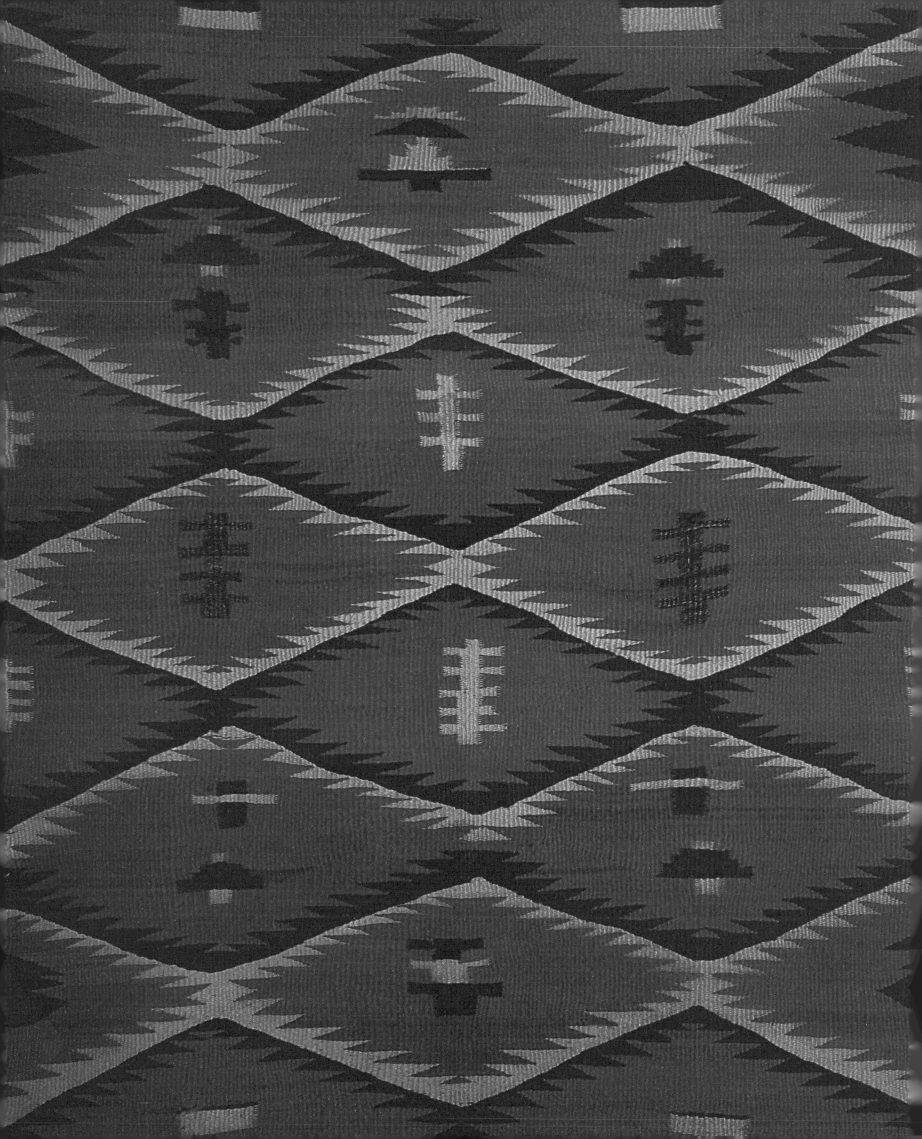

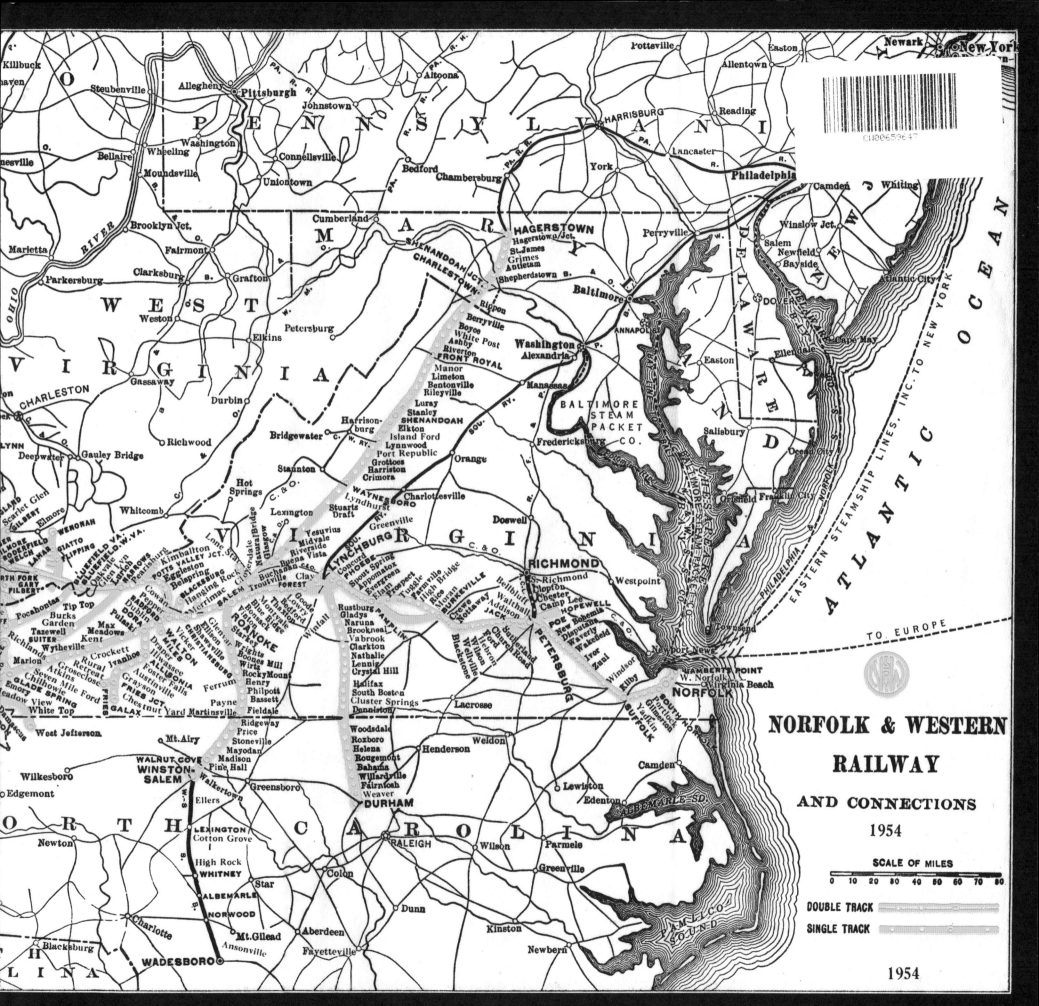

NORFOLK & WESTERN

RAILWAY

AND CONNECTIONS

1954

SCALE OF MILES

0 10 20 30 40 50 60 70 80

DOUBLE TRACK

SINGLE TRACK

1954

O. WINSTON LINK
LIFE ALONG THE LINE

A PHOTOGRAPHIC PORTRAIT OF AMERICA'S LAST GREAT STEAM RAILROAD

CLASS Y-6B IN THE WASH BAY AT BLUEFIELD. BLUEFIELD, WEST VIRGINIA,
JULY 27, 1955. NW 343

O. WINSTON LINK

LIFE ALONG THE LINE

A PHOTOGRAPHIC PORTRAIT OF AMERICA'S LAST GREAT STEAM RAILROAD

TONY REEVY

FOREWORD BY
SCOTT LOTHES

AFTERWORD BY
CONWAY LINK

ABRAMS, NEW YORK

CONTENTS

ELECTRICIAN J. W. DALHOUSE CLEANS
A HEADLIGHT. SHAFFERS CROSSING
ROUNDHOUSE, ROANOKE, VIRGINIA,
MARCH 19, 1955, NW 8

In Appalachia—where O. Winston Link photographed the Norfolk and Western Railway and also where I grew up—there is a long tradition of storytelling. On remote mountain farms in areas that lacked schools and even the means for writing, stories were often the only way of preserving heritage, just as people everywhere had done for millennia. The art of those stories was in the form of the telling and the retelling, which occurred almost exclusively at night. Part of the reason was practicality—there was no time for stories during the hard work of the day. But practicality was only part of it. The night shut out all other distractions, and in its void those stories could grow, and the listeners could contribute their own contextual imagery.

It is fitting that Winston Link applied this quality of the night to his momentous photography effort about the N&W. His engineering education and commercial photography experience provided an ideal background for both recognizing the potential for his night photos and executing them with theatrical brio. Artificial lighting allowed Link to include exactly—and only—what he wanted to include.

His critics, and even some of his admirers, find an argument here. By excluding the distractions, they say, he left out too much. Many of his photographs depict a hyperreality that is largely free of the grit we know to have existed in the small-town Appalachia of the late 1950s. But such a straight-up view was never Link's goal, and even in the art photography community such an approach would not become widely practiced until the New Topographics movement of the 1970s.

More than fifty years after Link made his last pictures on the N&W, his name has become synonymous with night railroad photography. Digital imaging, with its instant feedback and high sensitivities (offering sixteen times more light-gathering capability than the film Link used), has led to an explosion of amateur night photography. Many of today's practicing photographers, myself and uncounted other twenty- and thirty-somethings included, turn to Link's work when seeking ideas or inspiration for nocturnal views. His previous two books were among the first railroad photography books I owned, and they continue to occupy places on my shelves that are within easy reach. Those of us in the railroad photography community frequently and invariably draw comparisons to Link. It matters not that railroad and camera technology have changed drastically, that diesel locomotion replaced steam, and that many of today's young practitioners have never loaded film into a camera or picked up a flashbulb. If a recent railroad night photo is compelling, someone on an Internet discussion board will give it the Link stamp of approval. The cover story of the September 2008 issue of *Trains*, the nation's foremost railroad magazine, featured one of these current night photographers. The subtitle asked, "Is Gary Knapp the next O. Winston Link?"

Link's photographic legacy extends beyond American soil. One of his first major exhibitions occurred in London, and Germany has produced two of his greatest disciples, Axel Zwingenberger and Olaf Haensch. Steam lasted longer in Germany than it did in the United States, especially in the former East Germany, where steam continued in regular service on some lines into the 1990s. Many steam locomotives still operate on tourist railroads and special trains for enthusiasts. Zwingenberger and Haensch drew directly on inspiration from Link's work and embarked upon substantial, personally motivated night photography endeavors about Germany's steam trains. Neither had to wait decades for fame as Link did. Both published well-received books almost immediately that appeal to train-lovers and the general public alike: Zwingenberger's *Vom Zauber der Züge* (The Magic of Trains) in 2000, and Haensch's *NachtZüge* (Night Trains) in 2010.

Although he is most acclaimed for his night work, Link also made a substantial number of daytime photographs on the N&W, with many examples reproduced here. They prove, for one, that Link did not completely ignore the grittiness of Appalachia: See the hardscrabble life evinced in NW 119 (plate 138) and the proud but clearly impoverished Charlie Dollinger in NW 271 (plate 141). Link's daytime work along the Abingdon Branch is an iconic depiction of steam-era rural branch lines throughout the country; they touch us because whether we grew up in West Virginia, Wisconsin, or Oregon, we all feel that some ancestor or neighbor lived in towns like these and rode their own Virginia Creeper. On the main lines, Link's daytime work compares favorably to that of the best railfan photographers of his generation. The strong lines in the crossing scene of NW 48 (plate 82) and the over-the-cab view of two trains passing in NW 292 (plate 106) evoke the creativity of Richard Steinheimer, Jim Shaughnessy, and Philip R. Hastings.

But it was in the void of the night that Link created his most significant works, none more renowned than 1956's *Hotshot Eastbound* (NW 1103; see page 22). When the Nelson-Atkins Museum of Art in Kansas City mounted an international loan show of railroad art in 2008, *The Railway: Art in the Age of Steam*, curator Ian Kennedy chose Link to carry the banner for all American railroad photographers of the late steam era. Kennedy wrote that Link's photos "stand out among the vast and often distinguished corpus of post–[World War II] railway photography." While the show included several of Link's daytime photos, his most prominent was *Hotshot Eastbound*. The drive-in movie photo's pop culture fame includes a series in the comic strip *Gasoline Alley* (where Link received the pseudonym "O. Winken Blink") and a re-creation in a 1998 episode of *The Simpsons*, "Dumbbell Indemnity."

Even in the 1950s, Link was not alone as a night photographer of steam railroads. Steinheimer, Shaughnessy, Hastings, and others practiced night photography, experimenting with ambient light, open flash, and synchronized flash—occasionally with great success. The 2000 *Starlight on the Rails* exhibition at New York's Robert Mann Gallery presented some of their and their successors' best night work. Today, technological advances in both lighting equipment and digital imaging have made night photography easier than ever, and twenty-first-century railroad photographers, including some still in their teens, produce results that are sometimes stunning. Yet for all the night railroad photography that has followed Link's, his work remains the standard by which all of our efforts are judged.

Like Appalachia's tradition of storytelling, Link's photographs preserve and create memories. They have achieved international acclaim because they transcend geographic and generational boundaries, and even the locomotives themselves. For a century, the wailing whistle of a passing steam train—especially that of a night express—was the voice of progress, hopes and dreams, and escape, not only in America but also in much of the developed world. Link captured that voice—literally—in his sound recordings (some of the most lyrical and artistic ever made of railroad subjects). But he also found a way to convey that aural phenomenon through pictures that seem to talk, telling stories in the night.

Link's genius lay in looking at the region surrounding the Norfolk and Western Railway in Virginia, West Virginia, Maryland, and North Carolina in the late 1950s and finding what it was about that time and place that he wanted to remember for himself and wanted others to know and think about. His photographs continue to resonate—more than fifty years after he made the last one—because so many of us want to build the same memories and tease our imaginations with them. Our internal dialogues with his photographs, as with all art, occur inevitably and unbidden.

PREFACE
ENCOUNTERS WITH O. WINSTON LINK

In 1983, I was a summer intern at Glaxo Group Research in London, England, and was about to hike through Dartmoor, in Devon. I stopped by a map store in London and, as I was leaving, happened to notice railroad photos displayed in a window nearby. The images advertised an exhibition by a fellow American I had never encountered before: O. Winston Link. I paid the modest admission and viewed the exhibition with increasing excitement, and even joy. Here was a different way of looking at the railroad. It combined the human element that I had been seeking in railroad literature and photography with what was, to me, an undreamed-of weirdness in composition and an amazing technical virtuosity. I was especially taken by the photo titled *Cow #13, Silo, the Pocahontas #3, Man and Boy* (NW 723; see plate 111 for a similar photo).[1]

My next encounter with Link's legacy was my discovery, in 1988, of the Green Cove, Virginia, station and the Virginia Creeper Trail, and meeting the Edwards family—Karl and Adele and Adele's sister, Eleanor. They showed me and my girlfriend—now my wife, Caroline Weaver—the station and mentioned that a famous person, O. Winston Link, had been married there several years before. Adele spoke of him with great admiration, almost awe—she and Link were clearly close friends. After this visit, I went to the Arlington Public Library and found *Steam, Steel & Stars*, Link's first book, then about a year old. Both Caroline and I were entranced by the photos showcased in it. Over time, we became close friends with the Edwards family, and their daughter, Annette Goode, and her husband, Jim, remain friends of ours to this day.

In 1989, we drove from northern Virginia, where Caroline grew up and where we both lived at the time, to Roanoke, to see Link at a public appearance.

I have since written a great deal about Link and have talked about his work on occasion, including giving the keynote address at an O. Winston Link Museum function honoring the fiftieth anniversary of the first photo in Link's Norfolk and Western project, taken on January 21, 1955. In doing so, I have come to know a number of folks who were involved in his life—such as Tom Garver, David Plowden, the late Jim Boyd, and Kent Chrisman.

O. Winston Link died in 2001, but he is still remembered. He called the people of the Appalachian South "his people," and they reciprocated. My most memorable personal experience in this regard also happened at the Green Cove station. In the summer of 2003, exactly two decades after I stumbled on the Link exhibition in London, I was doing a reading from my first poetry chapbook, *Green Cove Stop*, at the station, which is now a visitors' center along the Virginia Creeper Trail. About half of the unexpectedly large audience was composed of locals, not something I had anticipated; nor, I suspect, had the event's sponsor, the U.S. Forest Service.

But the locals were not there to hear poems, such as the titular one from the chapbook, which is an ekphrastic poem based on one of Link's most famous images, *Old Maude Bows to the Virginia Creeper* (NW 1230; see opposite). What they wanted to hear was about O. Winston Link and his connection with the station, the site of several of his best daytime photos of the Norfolk and Western Railway in steam. Many of them had known him; many of them had prints of his images that had been given to them, or to their parents, as mementos after posing for one of his photos. Their admiration for Link was palpable. He always treated his subjects with respect, and in that wonderful part of the world, they return the feeling.

OLD MAUDE BOWS TO THE VIRGINIA CREEPER. GREEN COVE, VIRGINIA,
OCTOBER 27, 1956. NW 1230

INTRODUCTION
THE END OF STEAM

The 1950s in America is often viewed as a time of stasis, an interlude between the trials of the Great Depression and World War II and the upheavals of the 1960s and early 1970s. But a number of dramatic changes were taking place during the decade, alterations in the very fabric of our society that were to have sweeping consequences. One area of change, beginning in the 1940s but continuing through the 1950s and beyond, was the rise of the suburban growth pattern that still characterizes most of the United States today. Men (and women) returning from the horrors of World War II were anxious to nest in houses that developers were anxious to build. The result was the expansion of suburbia from prewar streetcar suburbs to vast tracts of automobile-dependent housing. The small, inexpensive ranch house became the suburban residence of choice, until growing American affluence led to its replacement with increasingly larger structures during the latter part of the twentieth century.

This development of modern suburbia was made possible by a transportation revolution. From about 1840 through World War I, the transportation required to develop the United States as a great nation spanning the North American continent was largely provided by the railroad. At the turn of the twentieth century—the "American Century"—competition appeared. The automobile and the airplane, which both began to rise to prominence in the early 1900s, eventually revolutionized passenger transportation. And the automobile's freight-transportation counterpart, the motor truck, joined the pipeline to forever alter how America's goods are transported.

The American railroad industry needed to evolve to survive. By the late 1940s, one of the changes that would eventually save it from ruin was well under way: the replacement of the labor-intensive steam locomotive by the diesel-electric locomotive. How-ever, traditions die hard in railroading, one of America's oldest and most entrenched industries. The transition to diesel, which started in earnest during the 1930s, was to span the 1940s and '50s, with the last fires in a steam locomotive on a major U.S. railroad not being dropped until the early 1960s.

The Norfolk and Western Railway, which encompassed a service area running from several large industrial centers in Ohio to the major port of Norfolk, Virginia, was one of the last railroads in North America to use steam locomotives. The reason was not a lack of imagination on the part of its management—in fact, the N&W (as it was often known) was a highly profitable subsidiary of the mighty, but then failing, Pennsylvania Railroad. The N&W would divorce itself from that dying colossus, easily survive the industry's difficulties in the 1950s through the 1970s, and eventually merge with another railroad to become Norfolk Southern Corporation, still a leading U.S. transportation company today.

Steam locomotion survived until May 1960 on the N&W for two principal reasons. First, like several other nearby rail lines, the Norfolk and Western was essentially a conveyor belt taking coal from mines in states such as West Virginia east to ships at Norfolk, and west, north, and south to Ohio, Pennsylvania, and North Carolina. The company was intimately connected to the coal industry and was loath to stop using coal as the fuel for its locomotives. Second, the N&W had used impressive internal engineering capabilities to roster four classes of locomotives—the Class J passenger engine, the Class A fast freight engine, the Class Y-6 heavy freight engine, and the Class S-1 and S-1a switch engines (originally developed for the Chesapeake & Ohio Railway)—that were arguably the best American steam locomotives ever built.

TRAIN #2 ARRIVES AT THE WAYNESBORO STATION. WAYNESBORO, VIRGINIA,
APRIL 14, 1955, NW 57

Nevertheless, by the mid-1950s the handwriting was on the wall for steam, even on the Norfolk and Western. Railroading was, and is, both a group of companies and a highly interconnected transportation system, and one corporation, even one as well led as the N&W, could not stand against the tide of change in the industry. Steam locomotives handled 78 percent of rail freight traffic in the United States in 1946 and were already down to just 31 percent by 1951. By 1959, the figure was less than 1 percent.[2]

The history of American railroading and the history of American photography are interlinked, and have been since the mid-nineteenth century. As a result, many photographers, from professionals to amateurs, followed the industry closely and documented it with numerous images. Many of the photographers interested in railroad subjects noted the coming end of steam on the American railroad and felt the steam locomotive and its setting should be documented before it ceased to exist. Railfan photographers such as Lucius Beebe, Charles Clegg, Philip R. Hastings, Jim Shaughnessy, and Richard Steinheimer stepped into the breach,[3] as did photographers with a firm sense of artistic purpose, such as Jack Delano, Walker Evans, and David Plowden. But as 1955 dawned, the man who made the most-noted photographs of twentieth-century American steam locomotives was about to discover the last days of steam on the Norfolk and Western.

O. WINSTON LINK

Ogle Winston ("O. Winston" or "Winston") Link was born in Brooklyn, New York, in 1914, and grew up at 483 Eighth Street in Brooklyn's Park Slope neighborhood. He retained the accent, and manner, of a Brooklynite throughout his life. But as is often true in the United States, his family's background is more complex than it may seem. His parents, Ernest Albert and Anne Winston Jones Link, were not native New Yorkers. Albert was born in Duffields, West Virginia, a small town in the Appalachian foothills near Harpers Ferry, on the Baltimore & Ohio Railroad (now CSX and MARC) line to Washington, D.C. Anne was born in Drewry's Bluff, Virginia, a small community near Richmond.[4] The background of Link's parents was later to prove critical to his artistry, as the family connections allowed him to claim the inhabitants of the American South, and of Appalachia, as his people. In fact, it seems likely that this background predisposed Link to form the obvious affection for western Virginia, northwestern North Carolina, and West Virginia that he developed during the Norfolk and Western project. This affection could have been artistically disastrous if it had led to sentimentality in his work, but instead it led him to a deepened feeling for his material—and that feeling is inherent in the quality and outlook of the photographs.

The Links had three children who lived to adulthood: Eleanor, Winston, and Albert Jr. Eleanor was older than Winston, and Albert Jr. was much younger. Appalachia and the South were very poor areas then, and the Links moved to New York to seek a better life. In the fashion of the times, Anne, who was a teacher, became a homemaker after she married. Albert taught manual arts (today referred to as vocational or occupational subjects). His expertise was an influence on Winston's interest in engineering, his quest for technical prowess in photography and other pursuits, and his love for artifacts of the Industrial Age.

O. Winston Link spent his life in the greater New York City area. He attended Manual Training High School, Merchants and Bankers Business and Secretarial School, and the Polytechnic

Institute of Brooklyn—often called "Brooklyn Poly" at the time, and now the Polytechnic Institute of New York University—graduating in 1937 with a degree in civil engineering.[5] This was in the depths of the Great Depression, and Link, unable to find an interesting opening in his field, took a position as a photographer with a large public relations firm, Carl Byoir & Associates.

Link's photographic experience before joining Byoir was limited. His father had encouraged his interest in photography, and before going to college, Winston had worked in a drugstore, printing photos. He also won a science prize for successfully photographing a solar eclipse.[6] While at Brooklyn Poly, he worked as a college newspaper photographer and also took photos of student engineering projects. In addition, he shot several weddings. But it was not this background that got Link his position: He was hired by Byoir on the basis of his comic imitation of a Brooklyn Poly mechanics of materials instructor. At a school banquet, Link, who was known for his practical jokes throughout his life, described photographing a local burlesque queen, but did it in the manner of this well-known professor. His routine brought down the house and attracted the attention of a Byoir executive who happened to be in the audience.[7]

Byoir handled public relations for clients such as B. F. Goodrich and Libbey-Owens-Ford, and Link was hired to take photographs of their products with enough pizzazz to get them published in newspapers and magazines. His most famous advertising photograph created for Byoir certainly had that pizzazz: It showed a model, wearing high heels and a bathing suit, standing on blocks of ice as a fire raged beneath her. Separating the fire from the ice is a sheet of Tuf-Flex glass produced by Libbey-Owens-Ford (see page 14).

O. WINSTON LINK IN HIS HOME. SOUTH SALEM, NEW YORK, 1995.
COURTESY OF MARY BACHMANN

LEFT A SELF-PORTRAIT ON ASSIGNMENT. NEW ORLEANS, LOUISIANA. 1937

RIGHT A FIRE-AND-ICE ADVERTISING PHOTOGRAPH TAKEN BY LINK FOR CARL BYOIR & ASSOCIATES' CLIENT LIBBEY-OWENS-FORD. 1938

Link's work for Byoir, and the aesthetic it instilled in him, placed him firmly in the posed advertising photography tradition, which was dominant in the field during the mid-1930s, when he was starting his professional photography career.[8] Link was to use posed tableaux in his best-known photographs of the Norfolk and Western in steam, most of them taken at night (although a review of the entire project shows that it is unfair to Link's artistry to claim that his work was confined to posed photographs, or to night images). Unfortunately, Link's advertising photographs, his typical images from this period, were works for hire that are scattered, usually unattributed, in period publications. They remain largely unstudied, with the exception of his photos of Louisiana.[9] These photos were saved from destruction by Winston's son, Conway Link, in the 1990s. Upon seeing them, Conway believed—and this observer would agree—that this body of Winston's commercial work has artistic value. The photos include images of alligator hunting, beekeeping, oil prospecting, and rice harvesting, as well as cotton crops, shrimp boats, and other subjects.

Link traveled on assignment for Byoir, often doing photography for clients in Texas and Louisiana. He remained with the firm for five years, from 1937 through 1942. During his tenure, while on assignment in Louisiana, he met the model Marteal Oglesby.[10] Winston and Marteal first encountered each other on the set of a Cecil B. DeMille film, *The Buccaneer*, where Marteal was doubling for the female lead Franciska Gaal.[11] They married in 1942.

World War II pulled Link, whose partial deafness made him unfit for military service, from Byoir to Columbia University's Airborne Instruments Laboratory in Mineola, New York, a secret installation working to develop an airborne submarine detector. He and Marteal then moved to nearby Hempstead, New York. Link worked at the laboratory from 1942 through its closing in 1945. While there, he developed prowess in night photography and mastered other technically demanding aspects of his craft. He would use this technical expertise, especially in lighting, combined with his experience in posed advertising photos, to create his night photos of the Norfolk and Western in steam.

According to Thomas H. Garver, then one of Link's assistants and now one of his foremost interpreters, Link's interest in capturing the American railroad at night developed while he worked at the laboratory.[12] Columbia's facility stood adjacent to the Long Island Rail Road, and Link's daily exposure to steam railroading rekindled a childhood interest in trains. A number of his daytime photos of steam-drawn trains on the Long Island Rail Road have been published and largely date from this period.[13] These photos show that Link did not confine his railroad-subject photography to the Norfolk and Western; unfortunately, like his advertising photography, his non-N&W railroad-subject photos have not yet been presented in a unified way as a body of work.[14]

In 1945, Marteal and Winston Link had their only child, son Winston Conway.[15] At about this time, with the Allies' victory in World War II, the Airborne Instruments Laboratory closed. Byoir invited Link back to the firm, but he decided to attempt a career as a freelance commercial photographer. He successfully developed a photography business with clients that included advertising agencies and corporations such as B. F. Goodrich, Alcoa, Texaco, and Ethyl. Link's marriage did not survive the stresses of starting a new career. Marteal and Winston separated in 1947 and divorced in 1948; Marteal returned to Louisiana, taking Conway with her. Winston initially ran his freelance business from his Hempstead home, but after the departure of his wife and child, he moved back to his parents' residence in Brooklyn.

At first, Link lived at his parents' home and used a friend's darkroom, but in 1949, he moved his workplace to a studio on East Thirty-fourth Street in Manhattan. He generally worked with only one or two part-time assistants, a roster that included at least three

A COMMERCIAL PHOTOGRAPH BY LINK

men critical to the story of the Norfolk and Western photographs: George Thom, Tom Garver, and David Plowden. This studio, and this business, was Link's grounding in life as he embarked on an ambitious, self-funded, and self-led attempt to document the last steam-powered railroad in America.

Although Link did not begin the Norfolk and Western project until 1955, he made a railroad night photo, using flashbulbs set in reflectors and connected to his camera's power supply, as early as 1946: a shot of a Missouri Pacific locomotive at Freeport Sulphur Company in Port Sulphur, Louisiana. At some point, probably in the mid-1950s, he submitted this photo to *Trains* magazine.[16]

Link started his freelance photography career in the 1940s, at the pinnacle of American industrial power. It is clear, even before Link undertook the task of documenting the last steam railroad in America, that, like many men of his generation, he had an interest in things classic and mechanical. As Tom Garver said, "Winston was never happier than when we pulled away from his studio on East 34th Street and headed south. We by-passed the proliferating franchise motels when we could, for Winston had a passion for the usable past—old buildings, old towns, old objects. He loved those things that were well and thoughtfully made and were mellow with use—in an era when nineteenth-century objects and buildings were regarded as failures of Victorian design."[17] Link's love for, and knowledge of, small towns and the technologies of the past was about to be put to the test as he created a body of art unique in the annals of American photography.

THE N&W PROJECT

In January 1955, O. Winston Link, on assignment in Staunton, Virginia, to photograph Westinghouse window-unit air conditioners, indulged his interest in trains by driving to nearby Waynesboro to find the tracks of the Norfolk and Western Railway. He had heard that the N&W was the last major American railroad operating entirely with steam locomotives.

In Waynesboro, Link found a very unusual, two-level depot. The Norfolk and Western tracks ran at ground level, and those of one of the line's archrivals, the Chesapeake & Ohio, passed over-

MISSOURI PACIFIC 4-6-0 #2325 SWITCHES AT FREEPORT SULPHUR COMPANY, PORT SULPHUR, LOUISIANA, 1946

head. A friendly telegrapher, Troy Humphries, who is featured in several of Link's finest photographs, invited Link to make himself at home.[18]

As Link looked around at the Waynesboro depot, with its cracked and puttied bay window, he realized he had stumbled upon what almost seemed to be a stage set for a Hollywood epic about the age of steam. Humphries faced a telegraph sounder and an ancient telephone, and the bay window ledge was ringed with telegraph relays. A depot clock with a wooden case hung on a beaded-board wall looped with wires, and the station's train order handles loomed next to the telegrapher's right arm. Beside the handles was a manual typewriter used for train orders and other station work. As Link visited with Humphries, a fast freight train led by a Norfolk and Western Class Y-6 locomotive halted at the depot, and then passenger Train #2—northbound for Hagerstown, Maryland, and New York—made its station stop.[19]

Link spent the next day photographing air conditioners in Staunton. That evening, he again drove to Waynesboro, bringing his 4 x 5 Graphic camera and some flash equipment. He and a helper made several photos, the first being NW 1 (*Train #2 Arrives at the Waynesboro Station*; plate 69). This photograph, the first in his Norfolk and Western series, was also the first to be published, in the August 1955 issue of *Trains* magazine.

After developing and printing these photos at his New York studio, Link envisioned a sweeping project—what Tom Garver has called "his own advertising campaign for the steam locomotive—and for the good life in small-town America."[20] Link's vision at this moment has proved to be a point of artistic genius, and he would likely be forgotten today—and our photographic record of the steam locomotive much diminished—if he had not developed this idea when he did.

Link was also fortunate to find a railroad management interested in preserving its company's history and the heritage of steam railroading. After he printed his Waynesboro photos, he wrote the Norfolk and Western's public relations department and posed his project:

Have you ever noticed the dearth of photographs of railroad scenes at night? I would like to make a series of well-planned night photographs of exceptional quality and interest showing the railroad at work as the passenger sleeps. For human interest, I would like to show an employee in every picture. On this proposed long-range project, all I could hope for from your railroad would be some sort of cooperation in picking locations and obtaining necessary permission to enter yards. Do you think your management would be favorable?[21]

The Norfolk and Western's management granted Link permission to take photos on its properties and even agreed to help him find suitable photo locations. In addition, Link went out on his own, sometimes riding N&W trains, to scout for suitable photo locations. According to Garver, Link rode most of the Norfolk and Western trackage in Virginia, West Virginia, and North Carolina during the spring and summer of 1955, using U.S. Geological Survey maps and other materials as guides to the landscape.[22]

As the project developed, the relationship between Link and Norfolk and Western employees, such as public relations executive Ben Bane Dulaney and president R. H. "Race Horse" Smith, deepened, and the cooperation between railroad company and photographer increased immensely. For example, it was Dulaney who suggested that Link photograph the Abingdon Branch,[23] the part of the N&W system and territory that Link would come to love best. Trains on the Abingdon Branch did not run at night, so this part of Link's Norfolk and Western project includes a large number of excellent daylight photos, many of them candid rather than posed shots.

Although it may be inaccurate to state that the N&W project is almost entirely composed of night photographs, it is certainly true that it is, with just a few exceptions, the night photos that the viewer tends to remember. Link deliberately focused on night shots, feeling that working at night would give him better control of the lighting on his subject while allowing him to eliminate unwanted elements from the image. "I can't move the sun, and I can't even move the tracks," was his comment about this strategy.[24] Clearly, a major reason for night photography in the context of this project was control, a need both personal and artistic. Also visible in the night photos is an emulation, whether conscious or unconscious, of contemporaneous atmospheric cinema such as film noir, and a recognition that black-metal, coal-fired, steam- and smoke-belching objects such as steam locomotives fit well in a night scene, and that the absence of color in the resulting images does not disadvantage these subjects.

Link's interest in Appalachia is also evident in the project. With the exception of a very few photos, the N&W images focus on Appalachian Maryland, West Virginia, Virginia, and North Carolina. Other very scenic portions of the N&W such as the "Pumpkin Vine"

branch (Roanoke, Virginia, to Winston-Salem, North Carolina) and the Durham branch (Lynchburg, Virginia, to Durham, North Carolina) are completely missing from the project.

As Link continued his Norfolk and Western project, he improved his lighting system. After taking the first photographs with limited lighting equipment, he used a parallel-wired system, and then a system wired in series and run by a battery-capacitor power supply that was innovative for its time (see page 202). These improvements allowed Link to take many of the tour de force night scenes that have become his signature images. For example, his retake of the Waynesboro scene, shot just a few months later (*Train #2 Arrives at the Waynesboro Station* [NW 57; see page 11]), added improved lighting and more human interest. When comparing NW 1 and NW 57, those preferring the constructed environment will probably be drawn to NW 57, while those with a minimalist eye may appreciate NW 1 for its more ghostly, less-staged quality.

Link would spend about $125,000 (in today's currency) of his own money on the project, and enough time to take more than twenty trips to the Norfolk and Western's service area.[25] His project, which spanned the years 1955 to 1960, ultimately produced more than 2,200 black-and-white and more than 400 color images and ended only when the N&W eliminated all steam engines. This set of images is possibly the best photographic treatment of the American steam-powered railroad and its milieu ever achieved. As far as we know, Link's railroad-subject photography came almost completely to a close when he ended his Norfolk and Western project.

This body of work was to deepen to include daytime photographs, a small amount of movie film, and—most famously—sound recordings. It was also to provide formative experience for writer, museum executive, and critic Tom Garver and renowned photographer David Plowden. Link's sound recordings were originally released as five 33⅓ rpm long-playing records, as well as a 45 rpm record not related to the N&W project. Ironically, in view of his present position as an icon of American photography, these recordings were better known than his photographs, from the release of his first album in 1957 until he burst onto the American and British art photography scenes in 1983. A number of notable, unpublished recordings made by Link as part of his Norfolk and Western project, provided on a CD with accompanying notes, are included with this book. Many of them were made at the exact time and location of some of the photographs featured here.

In addition to making sound recordings during this period, Link also sought outlets for his photos, and his images were eventually featured in a few significant publications. *Trains* editor David P. Morgan ran two articles in 1957 that were highly influential with railfan photographers[26] and also featured a number of single photos from the N&W project, including the first-known publication of any of the images, soon after the project started in 1955. Morgan thought enough of Link's photography to include him in one of his two mid-1950s "Photo Section" features showcasing (in Morgan's view) the greatest railroad-subject photographers published in *Trains* at that time.[27] The N&W's corporate magazine, *Norfolk and Western Magazine*, published an article about Link's work in 1956, with copy attributed to Ben Bane Dulaney; and in 1957, the railroad issued a booklet, *Night Trick*, featuring a number of Link's best N&W night photos taken up to that point. The booklet is undated and has no byline, but the copy is also attributed to Dulaney. *Night*

Trick, still fairly common and often bought and sold on the railfan market today, remained the only available monograph featuring Link's N&W images for almost thirty years.

Link was the subject of one known exhibit during the period of the project, the self-curated *Stop, Look & Listen*, presented at his Manhattan studio from May to September 1956. This was the only documented one-person exhibit Link would have until 1983. David Morgan attended the exhibit, as did N&W engineer Walter Finney.[28] Link wanted the exhibit to be what we would today call a multimedia event, and his wish to play sound recordings of N&W steam in the background led him to begin his series of Norfolk and Western sound recordings.

In 1958, the N&W changed management, and R. H. Smith was replaced by Stuart Saunders, who was later to achieve infamy

GHOST TOWN. STANLEY, VIRGINIA. FEBRUARY 1, 1957. NW 1345

with his role in the Penn Central bankruptcy. The new management was less supportive of Link's project, although they still assisted him to some extent. Indeed, by viewing the N&W photos in chronological order, one can see that the quality of the images declined at about this time, and then rebounded at the very end of the project, in late 1959 and early 1960. Link stated that "A new bunch of bosses came in, and they grew impatient with me to finish the whole business."[29]

Link's last field trip in connection with his Norfolk and Western project was March 7 to March 19, 1960.[30] The last steam run on the N&W occurred on May 6, 1960.[31]

LINK'S JOURNEY TO FAME

O. Winston Link remained active as a commercial photographer until the early 1980s. He was known in the rail-enthusiast community for his albums of sound recordings and a scattering of photographs in *Night Trick*, in *Trains* magazine, and later, in several books. The end of exposure in *Trains* left Link's Norfolk and Western images largely in limbo. Although they would inspire other railroad-subject photographers, they seemed to have little appeal to rail-enthusiast publishers during the 1960s and '70s. Lucius Beebe and Charles Clegg used three of the N&W photos in the 1964 limited-release *Great Railroad Photographs, U.S.A.* and published two more in *The Trains We Rode: Volume II* (1966). In the early 1970s, railfan writer and photographer Don Ball published several N&W images as well.

Link continued to conduct very time-consuming and expensive projects following the end of his Norfolk and Western project. He acquired a Canadian Pacific Railway steam engine and a Rutland Railroad combine (a railroad car with both a passenger seating section and a baggage compartment) and spent three decades trying to restore them on his own. Much later, Norfolk Southern Corporation gave Link a surplus caboose. Link restored the combine, which was acquired from his estate by the Railway Historical Society of Northern New York. It is held in storage by the Society.[32] Link was ultimately unable to restore the locomotive. It was purchased in 2011 by a rail enthusiast in Virginia and will be cosmetically restored for permanent display.

Link also continued to conduct subject-specific photography projects. Soon after his work with the N&W ended, he undertook

STOP, LOOK & LISTEN, AN EXHIBIT OF LINK'S N&W PHOTOGRAPHY. NEW YORK, NEW YORK, JUNE 1, 1956, NW 1060

a self-funded project documenting construction of the Verrazano-Narrows Bridge, which connects Brooklyn and Staten Island in New York City. He was ultimately able to recoup a portion of his costs by selling some of this work. This project led to a commission to photograph all of the New York City bridges managed by the Triborough Bridge and Tunnel Authority (TBTA). This photography was intended to result in a book published by the Authority, but the project was dropped when the TBTA became a part of New York's Metropolitan Transportation Authority.[33] In 1969, Link moved his studio to a smaller location on Park Avenue South in Manhattan.

Jim Boyd, the longtime editor of *Trains* competitor *Railfan* (later *Railfan & Railroad*), gave Link a break in 1976 by writing and publishing the first major retrospective article about him, titled "Master of the Night." This article is very technical and remains one of the best descriptions of Link's night photography procedure and technology. Boyd also assigned Link a night shot of the Lehigh & Hudson River Railway near Warwick, New York, published as the cover of the same issue. Boyd noted in a later *Railfan & Railroad* article that Link's prickly personality and stringent rights policies did not help his publications record. "When I first met Winston Link in New York City in the early 1970s," Boyd said, "he was rather embittered that 'nobody remembered' what he had done. I probably was not alone in pointing out that he had produced only one very small book and a few record albums up to that time and was rather difficult to deal with in getting his photos for publication."[34]

During the mid-1970s, Link achieved his first major success in the art world. At the urging of his friend Salem Tamer (later a trustee of the O. Winston Link Revocable Trust), Link sought out John Szarkowski, then director of the Museum of Modern Art's photography department. Tom Garver provided a letter of introduction of Link to Szarkowski. In 1976, Szarkowski purchased five of Link's photos for the museum, and Link gifted a sixth.[35] Szarkowski later said of Link's photography, "It was an absolute virtuoso performance. His work has a strangeness and nostalgia that is remarkable."[36]

In 1982 and 1983, Link became arguably the first contemporary railroad-subject photographer to break out of the commercial and/or railfan photography scenes and into the world of art photography.[37] In doing so, he won, as far as we can tell from our

GHOST TRAIN. TIME FREIGHT #83 WESTBOUND OVER BRIDGE 5. NORFOLK, VIRGINIA, 1955, NW 419A

vantage point in time, lasting fame. The distribution of his images in the art world has also brought them to the attention of other photographers, and some critics see his work as an influence on noted photographers leading a revival of the great American tradition of posed art, advertising, and portrait photography—perhaps in reaction to the "street photography" of artists such as Robert Frank.

What led to Link's breakout, and why did it take three decades? First, it is important to note that, until recent years, photographs were not valued, financially or artistically, in the way that paintings and other fine art have long been. This is largely because photography as a fine art movement began to reach maturity only in the 1970s and 1980s. As photographs gained value as art objects, it became worthwhile for critics, academics, gallery owners, and collectors to seek out unknowns whose work seemed to have

HOTSHOT EASTBOUND, IAEGER, WEST VIRGINIA,
AUGUST 2, 1956, NW 1103

artistic content and value. Until this time, Link was on the margins, and not just because he was not well known. The range of interest in the medium, according to photography historian Bill Johnson, had to grow to include photographers such as Link:

First, the monetary value of photographs had to increase until it was worthwhile for someone to search out the person in the margins. By the early 1980s, a number of people were successfully creating a market for photography. Second, as broad interest in photography grew, a movement that started after World War II and really took off in the late 1960s, the range of interest in photography naturally grew as well. Until then [the early 1980s], Link was overlooked because he was commercial and not the right kind of commercial—not a photojournalist, not a fashion photographer. Also, he was making photographs advocating a reinterpretation of mid-America that was frowned on in Eastern elitist circles. His work awaited the attention of a curator looking for something new that they could do, and that they could afford and collect—like Carolyn Carr at the Akron Art Museum. And there's some level of luck to a discovery like that—somebody sees something, gets interested, and puts time into it.[38]

In 1982, Link was profiled in a long article in *American Photographer* and was featured in his first group exhibition, *Floods of Light: Flash Photography, 1851–1981*, organized by the Photographers' Gallery in London. Two exhibition directors, Rupert Martin at the Photographers' Gallery and Carolyn Carr of the Akron (Ohio) Art Museum, simultaneously and, apparently, independently, organized Link exhibitions, both of which opened in 1983. The exhibits resulted in catalogs, giving more people access to Link's railroad-subject images. In Martin's case, the curator was so moved by Link's photos, which he saw when overseeing *Floods of Light*, that he was inspired to begin planning the 1983 exhibition.

Why did Martin and Carr choose to champion Link's work? Martin's comments about Link at the time suggest why the photographs appealed to him. "I've never seen anything like his work," he said. "It's unique and it works on several different levels. It works for railway buffs, for people interested in photography, and then there's the strictly human level. His pictures allow you to involve yourself in the lives of Americans in the 1950s."[39]

Moreover, beginning in the late 1960s, critics began to develop an interest in commercial photography—works created for purely utilitarian purposes—and in whether such works could have artistic value. This movement was perhaps accelerated by the rise of "constructed reality" photographers such as Cindy Sherman and Laurie Simmons, whose photographs reflected advertising images of the 1950s, as well as filmic influences. Although Link's Norfolk and Western series was not created for commercial purposes—in fact, it was created as a result of Link's personal vision—he was known in the photography community only as a hired gun: a freelance commercial photographer. This had, until then, and to Link's great frustration, kept him outside the pale of the art photography world. He may not have been interested in contemporary art and art photography, but the recognition and financial success that the art photography community offered certainly appealed to him. It also seems certain that Link was, up until about this time, unfamiliar with, if not ignorant of, how the world of fine art, galleries,

museums, and so on worked. This made it even harder for him to break into it. Link's new wife, Conchita Mendoza, whom he married in 1984, clearly helped him with this transition, as did Tom Garver and Salem Tamer.

Another thing that helped Link gain recognition was time—for at least two reasons. First, as he did his work, stemming from the posed advertising photography tradition, street photographers such as Robert Frank[40] and Henri Cartier-Bresson swept the art photography world, and the small 35mm camera made taking quickly composed images possible. Link was not entirely comfortable with this technique, and its popularity rendered his images out of step with the times in the art photography world of the 1950s. As seems inevitable in art, a reaction to this movement set in, and artists of note, such as Jeff Wall, arose. These artists looked back to the posed tradition. The success these and other similar photographers enjoyed, beginning in the late 1970s, paved the way for O. Winston Link's recognition soon thereafter.

Second, as time passed, American society also looked back at Link's subjects with affection and nostalgia. Small towns and the steam locomotive were simply part of the American cultural background in 1955. By 1983—even before Walmart really challenged the small-town store—much of rural America was in decline, and recent college graduates, for example, were too young to have experienced steam engines in regular railroad service. The railroad itself had gone from the major carrier of passengers, express packages, and mail in the United States to a behind-the-scenes hauler of bulk freight, making images of a time when American society was dependent upon the railroad, and the railroad was integral to that society, new and challenging, rather than commonplace. Link's photographs, which were specifically posed to reflect small towns and steam locomotion, appealed to a changed nation nostalgic for its past. Clearly, with the locations Link chose, he purposely emphasized small-town and rural life in the Norfolk and Western's service area, avoiding cities along the railroad such as Norfolk, Virginia. Commercial photographer and Link associate Ben Halpern feels that Link sought to rejuvenate the image of small-town America by showing "a very pure way of life that had been unchanged for a long time. . . . He referred to the people in his photos as his people. Notice that everyone looks comfortable and middle-class. You don't see any tension or unhappiness, even among the teenagers. Many of the people don't even look at the locomotives passing by; they are having too much fun going about their daily activities."[41]

In this respect, Link reflected the N&W's own corporate public relations material, which referred to its service area (including the coal-mining regions of western Virginia and West Virginia) as the "Land of Plenty." In short, the content of Link's Norfolk and Western project didn't just create an advertisement for the steam-powered railroad in the United States; it also sought to showcase the Norman Rockwell–like qualities, as the photographer saw them, of life in the small towns along the railroad.

As with any lasting creative work, there are debates among critics about the photos themselves, their artistic worth, and Link's goals as an artist. Tom Garver has insisted that the artistic and social content that many see in the photos was unintentional. The Norfolk and Western series, he has stated, was a project to preserve views of the last steam railroad in America. It was solely intended to document the passing of what many consider to be America's most beautiful machine and to record the small towns

that thrived along the corridor that it and its employer, the railroad industry, created. Garver said:

Link never articulated his intention in doing the Norfolk and Western project, but I believe he saw it as something different he could do to overcome the anonymity of being an advertising photographer. Link had a great need to achieve something significant. I believe he also felt a deep-seated need to preserve the era of steam railroading. What he accomplished is that he created his own advertising campaign for the steam locomotive—and for the good life in small-town America. . . . In the end, he was selling a dream—the dream of the steam locomotive in America.[42]

However, many observers—Rupert Martin, Carolyn Carr, John Szarkowski, *New York Times* critic Andy Grundberg, and other photographers—have seen even more in the photos. As Bill Johnson noted, they "hold their own weight" and are viewed now as art objects rather than as merely documentary images. And, as Johnson also noted, despite what nostalgia has done for Link's reputation, there is a "weird feeling" in the photographs, as in the photography of Edward Weston and Ansel Adams, that Link was "working out of, beyond, time"—meaning, perhaps, that "the subject matter [of the photographs] was secondary to the artist's vision of it."[43] Critics such as Robin Updike of the *Seattle Times* and Arturo Silva of the *Daily Yomiuri* have characterized Link's work as surreal, even uncanny.[44]

Tom Garver objects strongly to the notion of applying the tag "surreal" to Link's images, and in the technical sense of the term, he is probably correct.[45] But what about in the popular sense of the word? What are we to make, for example, of the Hawksbill Creek image (*Hawksbill Creek Swimming Hole* [NW 1128]; see plate 119 for a variant), which shows five children—four of them quite small, and an attractive teenage girl—splashing vigorously in a stream on a summer night, and long after the little ones' bedtimes? Clearly, after stimulating such a high level of artistic debate and interest, Link's photos have earned their place and do stand as works of art.

The 1983 exhibitions brought out a theme that was echoed in John R. Stilgoe's book *Metropolitan Corridor*, which was published the same year—namely, that it was no longer enough to examine railroads from a mechanical standpoint. Railroading was developed by, and affected, people, as well as the natural and built environment. Both Link's photos and Stilgoe's revisionist look at the built environment created by the railroad in the United States supported the notion that the social and cultural aspects of railroading were, and are, fertile fields for study.

The 1983 Akron Art Museum exhibit of Link's N&W images traveled to New York's International Center of Photography. This resulted in an influential review of Link's photography by Andy Grundberg in the *New York Times*,[46] which celebrated Link's use of flashbulbs to produce a "thoroughly delightful aura of strangeness." Grundberg pointed out that Link could achieve his effect thanks to the railroad itself, "by the way the tracks ran through backyards and down main streets and past drive-in movie theaters," and by the willingness of railroad workers and local residents to cooperate in his "elaborate simulations."

Just after the 1983 exhibitions is when Link married Conchita Mendoza. The couple were married at the Green Cove, Virginia, railroad station, the subject of one of Link's most famed photographs—and his most recognized daytime photo, *Old Maude Bows to the Virginia Creeper* (NW 1230; see page 9). The Links then built a home on a lot that Winston had long owned, on Lake Rippowam, in South Salem (Westchester County), New York. Conchita acted as Winston's manager for many years, and sales of his prints, and his print prices, increased dramatically. By this time, Link's reputation had gained critical mass, and in 1987, his long-awaited first book, *Steam, Steel & Stars: America's Last Steam Railroad*, was issued.

"A FAIRY-TALE ENDING DERAILED" [47]

A strange period in Link's life ensued. *Steam, Steel & Stars* was well received, and his fame was increasing. A 1990 documentary directed by Paul Yule, *O. Winston Link: Trains That Passed in the Night*, was released. His steam engine was delivered to a shop in Rome, New York, for a full restoration. But at the same time, his marriage to Conchita was dissolving, and in the worst possible way. Apparently, Conchita had told Link's contacts in the art world that he had Alzheimer's disease; and while he printed and signed hundreds of now-valuable photographs in the basement of their home, she had an affair with Ed Hayes, the head of the shop working on Link's locomotive, and stole most of the proceeds from the sales of Link's photos. The situation led to the couple's bitter divorce in 1993. In 1995, Conchita was charged with grand larceny for allegedly stealing a number of Link's photographs. She was convicted in 1996, was sentenced to prison, and was paroled in 2000.[48]

With respect to developing an understanding of Link's oeuvre, this controversy is a double-edged sword. On the one hand, the notoriety of the case actually led to increased interest in Link's photography and expanded the sale and value of his prints. But the bizarre nature of the case, and the unresolved matters swirling around it,[49] tend to distract attention from the critical factor: Link's lifework.

Link's last years were bittersweet. On the one hand, issues relating to his divorce and the actions of his ex-wife continued to haunt him. On the other hand, he was idolized by the people of Roanoke, Virginia, and other areas that he had photographed, as well as by railfans and art collectors and critics. A second book, *The Last Steam Railroad in America*, with a narrative by Tom Garver, was issued in 1995. Link made a cameo appearance in *October Sky*, a major motion picture released in 1999, and by the time of his death on January 30, 2001, negotiations were under way to establish a museum in Roanoke as a home for his work.

After his divorce from Conchita, Link rekindled a friendship with Ben Bane Dulaney's stepdaughter, Joan Thomas, whom he had known during the 1950s, when she was a teenager. Joan assisted with the distribution of Link's sound recordings, which led to a revival of interest in that portion of Link's Norfolk and Western project. They remained close until Link's death.[50]

Link is buried in his family's plot in Elmwood Cemetery, Shepherdstown, West Virginia, near his father's birthplace in Duffields. His grave lies close to the sites of a number of his noted photos of the Norfolk and Western's Shenandoah Valley line.

The controversy surrounding Link's second marriage outlived him. Three years after Conchita's release from prison, she and Ed Hayes (whom she had since married) were caught in a sting operation when they attempted to sell more of Link's photos. This led to the discovery of Hayes's rented storage area, which contained a trove of Link's prints. The two spent a year in jail awaiting trial, and in 2004, both pleaded guilty to possession of stolen goods. Hayes was released for time served, but Conchita received a prison sentence.[51]

A MUSEUM IS FOUNDED

Link was approached several times by entities wishing to provide a home for his Norfolk and Western project, but he was never satisfied with the proposals he received. In 1999, Norfolk Southern Corporation executive David Helmer approached Kent Chrisman, executive director of the Historical Society of Western Virginia, about the possibility of a Link museum in the former N&W headquarters city of Roanoke. Chrisman and Jim Sears, president and general manager of the Western Virginia Foundation for the Arts and Sciences, the developer of Roanoke's downtown Center in the Square, liked the idea. In 2000, a contingent from Roanoke visited Link, who was supportive of the planned museum.

It was Link who suggested, among other locations, the former Roanoke N&W passenger station. The station, then vacant and already shorn of its concourse, is an important artifact in its own right: It was built at the turn of the twentieth century and then remodeled into high-modern style in the late 1940s, using a design by a firm led by another famed artist of the American rails, Raymond Loewy. In the late 1990s, Norfolk Southern donated the station to the Roanoke Foundation for Downtown.

By August 2001, the museum group had successfully negotiated the purchase of Link's Norfolk and Western negatives and a set of prints, as well as his notes and lighting equipment, from the trustees of the O. Winston Link Revocable Trust—friend Salem

Tamer and son Conway Link. Meanwhile, the Western Virginia Foundation for the Arts and Sciences acquired the Roanoke station in 2000 and began renovating it, raising $6.6 million for the project. The restored station then provided a site for the O. Winston Link Museum and for the Roanoke Valley Convention & Visitors Bureau, which occupies the former ticket lobby and baggage-check room. The O. Winston Link Museum Committee, led by David Helmer and another volunteer, John P. Bradshaw Jr., raised $2.8 million to establish the museum within the restored station.

Tom Garver served as the museum's founding curator on a consulting basis, writing much of the copy featured in the exhibits when the museum opened in January 2004. He also helped develop the conceptual idea for the museum. Garver was well qualified, beyond his personal connection to Link, to provide consulting services for this and other museums. He now serves as an independent curator and exhibition organizer and continues to write about art and the history of technology in America. The museum published a booklet, *O. Winston Link: The Man and the Museum*, with text by Garver. After *Steam, Steel & Stars* and *The Last Steam Railroad in America* went out of print, this booklet kept Link's legacy in print for several years.

It is likely that more of Link's work remains to be discovered. In recent years, Conway Link developed an interest in his father's late-1930s images of Louisiana, and so those photos have received critical attention. A number of them, such as *Cramped Quarters*, *Traders on the Floor*, and *Net Repair*, are of exceptionally high artistic quality. It is interesting to speculate how much of Link's photography beyond the Norfolk and Western and Louisiana portfolios survives, and whether it is artistically significant.

INFLUENCES AND THOSE INFLUENCED

It has often been noted that Link's major influences were other commercial photographers in the grand, posed tradition of his day, as well as the nineteenth-century prints of Currier and Ives. The Currier and Ives influence is undeniable. In particular, the influence of prints that Link owned is very obvious in some of his photographs, such as *The Birmingham Special Westbound Passing Max Meadows Station* (NW 1622).[52] The general influence of advertising

THE BIRMINGHAM SPECIAL WESTBOUND PASSING MAX MEADOWS STATION. MAX MEADOWS, VIRGINIA. DECEMBER 22, 1957. NW 1622

photography, which attempts to sell a product by projecting feel-good images, is also present.

But it is difficult to believe that these were Link's only influences.[53] The paintings of Edward Hopper have often been mentioned, but cannot be substantiated, as a possible source of inspiration. Several critics have also seen similarities between Link's photographs and the paintings and illustrations of Norman Rockwell, which would have been familiar to Link through their frequent, prominent placement on the cover of the *Saturday Evening Post*. It

is interesting to note that Hopper and Link were contemporaneous, although Link was much younger, and that they were almost neighbors: Hopper was from Nyack, New York, across the Hudson River from the area where Link lived the last years of his life. Hopper's studio was in New York City, as was Link's. And Hopper's first major retrospective was held in New York's Museum of Modern Art in 1933; Link was a teenager living in Brooklyn at the time. It is difficult not to see the influence of precisionist photographer and painter Charles Sheeler in Link's photography, although Link's knowledge of Sheeler's images cannot be substantiated either. Critics have also compared Link's photographs to those of seminal nineteenth-century landscape photographers such as William Henry Jackson and A. J. (Andrew Joseph) Russell, who often included trains in their work. These photographers, of course, were contemporaneous with Currier and Ives.

Recent scholarship has tended to minimize the influence of the Farm Security Administration (FSA) photographers, such as Marion Post Wolcott and Walker Evans, during the years the FSA and its successor, the Office of War Information (OWI), were active (the Great Depression and World War II).[54] The breakout event for the FSA photographers, arguably, was the exhibit *The Bitter Years*, organized by Edward Steichen for the Museum of Modern Art in 1962, after the end of Link's Norfolk and Western project. But we must recall that Link was a commercial photographer, and one of the key upscale markets for business-oriented print advertisements during the 1940s, '50s, and '60s was *Fortune* magazine, a New York–based periodical founded in 1930 by Henry Luce (of *Time*, *Life*, and "The American Century" fame). Evans, a photographer who worked for the FSA[55] from 1935 to 1937, went on to be a staff

HESTER FRINGER'S LIVING ROOM ON THE TRACKS.
LITHIA, VIRGINIA, DECEMBER 16, 1955. NW 720

photographer at *Fortune* from 1945 to 1965.[56] His fame earned him a position at the magazine that allowed him freedom to produce a number of excellent portfolios, including four focused on the American railroad.[57] One of these, "The U.S. Depot," published in February 1953, contains views that resemble some of Link's[58] and were an obvious and acknowledged influence on David Plowden, who worked for Link and then became Evans's protégé.[59] The final of these four was "The Last of Railroad Steam," published in September 1958, a series of views of Norfolk and Western steam as it was being phased out. Although it's not known if Link read *Fortune*, as a highly competitive New York–based commercial photographer, he is likely to have done so, and therefore it is possible that he saw Walker Evans's images. It is also interesting to note that Evans's *Walker Evans: American Photographs*, considered one of the most important American photography books of the twentieth century, was issued by New York's Metropolitan Museum of Art in 1938. *Walker Evans: American Photographs* was the catalog to an exhibition of the same name that appeared at the Museum of Modern Art in New York, also in 1938. Link, of course, lived and worked in New York at that time.

Link was an enthusiastic contributor to the most influential railfan publication, *Trains* magazine, and there is no doubt that he read this periodical and corresponded with editor David P. Morgan. Although critics such as Tom Garver have stated that Link was not influenced by railfan photographers,[60] it is interesting to note that several pioneering night photographers who focused their lenses on American railroading—Richard Steinheimer, Jim Shaughnessy, and Philip R. Hastings—were featured prominently in *Trains* during the 1950s. Many of their photos resemble Link's, although these

men lacked the resources to put together a synchronized flash system as large as his, so their night photography is less technically impressive.[61] Shaughnessy, who largely focused on railroad subjects, is a pioneer of open-flash, time-exposure photography in general. Even though Link did not mention being influenced by these men, there is little doubt that he saw their images as he flipped through issues of *Trains*. Given Link's obvious interest in railroads, it seems reasonable to assume that he was influenced by the magazine's emerging style of action photography. Moreover, Morgan's intense chronicling of the steam locomotive as it faded from mainline railroading, in articles usually accompanied by Hastings's photographs, would have struck a responsive chord as Link pursued his own project to document the last major U.S. railroad to resist the diesel revolution.

In overview, it seems unwise to assume, at face value, that Link was not influenced by anything beyond fellow commercial photographers and Currier and Ives prints. The common view of Link is that he lacked influences from the world of art and was unaware of fine art photographers and even of noted railroad-subject photographers. Observers of Link's work may be taking the persona of an artistically unaware commercial photographer, created by Link and his advocates as he entered the world of fine art photography, as fact rather than personal statement. An artist has the right to create a persona, but those who come after him have the right to question it. It is clear that Link had personae: Contrast the crusty Brooklynite—who could be distant, even negative, with those he saw as possible competitors, such as David Plowden—that fellow New Yorkers experienced, with the genial eccentric who developed a relationship of mutual admiration and affection with "his people," the folks of Appalachia. To assume Link, a brilliant commercial photographer living in one of the world centers of artistic endeavor, was not influenced by his surroundings is naive. It is especially so when one considers the echoes of the work of artists such as Walker Evans, Edward Hopper, Charles Sheeler, and the photographers associated with *Trains* magazine.

While Link's influences remain unclear, his influence is more easily defined. He is seen as a pioneer in the field of night photography. Longtime *Railfan & Railroad* editor Steve Barry, himself a noted photographer of railroad subjects, said:

> Link was a pioneer, and was years ahead of his time. He used night photography to create drama and, like his contemporaries Phil Hastings and Jim Shaughnessy, realized that depicting the railroad at night allowed a familiar subject to take on new dimensions. Like Hastings and Shaughnessy, he went beyond the railroads to including cars, people and houses in his shots. What almost nobody has been able to duplicate is the technical quality of his work and, given the changes in the culture of railroading and the unavailability of flashbulbs, it may never be duplicated. In fact, I believe Link's work is the most outstanding photography of steam that we have.[62]

Despite the paucity of Link's work available to photographers until 1983, his *Night Trick* pamphlet and the articles in *Trains* had a direct influence on three well-known railfan photographers and one group of photographers: Mel Patrick, Ted Benson, Jim Boyd (the *Railfan* editor who championed Link's photography in 1976), and Rails After Dark (Howard Pincus, Bob Hart, and Al Papp), who used synchronized lighting in their railroad-subject night photographs. These photographers are little known outside rail-enthusiast circles.

On the other hand, Jim Shaughnessy's work has entered the world of fine art photography, and he acknowledges Link as a major influence. Shaughnessy used Link's photography as an inspiration in taking several of his best-known photographs.[63] Jeff Brouws, coauthor of a survey of railroad-subject night photography published in 2000, *Starlight on the Rails*, and the author of a book on Richard Steinheimer, has in recent years also championed Shaughnessy's work. This collaboration resulted in *The Call of Trains: Railroad Photographs by Jim Shaughnessy*, an art photography book published in 2008.

Link's Norfolk and Western images, as a number of critics and interpreters have pointed out, are inherently different from the work of railfan photographers such as Shaughnessy, Hastings, Patrick, and Boyd. Although a locomotive, train, or railroader is generally present in Link's N&W photographs, it is sometimes not emphasized (consider, for example, the value of the cows and the silo versus that of the distant train in *Train #77 Westbound* [NW 722; plate 111], or the glimpse of the locomotive through the living room window versus the focus on the mother, son, and family pets in *Hester Fringer's Living Room on the Tracks* [NW 720; see page 28]. Rather, the railroad is present in the way a recurrent theme is in a great novel or piece of music; Link used it brilliantly as a way to tie his portfolio of small-town life in southern Appalachia together. The result is both technical and artistic mastery in a single body of work.

David Plowden, one of Link's assistants, was to achieve similar artistic mastery through a body of work focusing on the changing American landscape and the destruction of much of its historically built environment. Plowden's photography is formalist, owing much more artistically to the photography of Walker Evans than it does to Link's. However, Link's obsession with documenting the last of steam represents an intellectual transfer to Plowden and led, along with other influences, to Plowden's excellent work on the end of Canadian Pacific steam (1959 and 1960), his documentation of the last steam-powered boats and ships in America throughout his career, and other images. Plowden has long since gained recognition as an American photographer of artistic significance, initially for his environmental photography and his depiction of American bridges. His railroad-subject photography gained recognition with the 1987 publication of the book *A Time of Trains*, and attention to this body of his work was heightened with the 2010 publication of *Requiem for Steam: The Railroad Photographs of David Plowden*. Still active in his late seventies, Plowden is an important figure carrying on Link's passion to record the vanishing icons of traditional American culture. The younger photographers carrying on this tradition include Jeff Brouws, Joel Jensen, and Mark Ruwedel.

Link's most significant influence on American photography, however, transcends railroad-subject photography. His images, complex tableaux, are a major influence on the "constructed reality" movement in contemporary American photography.[64] This movement stems from the conceptual art movement of the 1960s and '70s.

For a line of work in the constructed reality genre that reflects Link's influence, one should look to the complex tableaux of Jeff Wall and Gregory Crewdson, artists who acknowledge Link as an artistic ancestor.[65] Wall, a writer and an academic as well as a photographer, has not only created some of the best-known con-

structed reality photographs but also has provided, through his writings, much of the philosophic underpinning for this genre of photography. His images range from portraits to still lifes to complex tableaux. It is in the latter images that one sees Link's influence most clearly. Many comparisons between their works are possible. One example is Wall's *Eviction Struggle* (1988); the exaggerated poses of the models in this image are reminiscent of the most obviously posed of Link's night photos, such as *The Grottoes Volunteer Fire Department Answers a Call* (NW 1349; see below). Another comparison is between Wall's *The Drain* (1989) and the previously mentioned *Hawksbill Creek Swimming Hole* (NW 1128; plate 119).[66]

Gregory Crewdson, who is, like Link, from Brooklyn's Park Slope neighborhood, first debuted as a punk rock musician. His surreal photographs depict his view of small-town and suburban

THE GROTTOES VOLUNTEER FIRE DEPARTMENT ANSWERS
A CALL. GROTTOES, VIRGINIA, FEBRUARY 10, 1957, NW 1349

America. Edward Hopper and Diane Arbus are obvious influences on his work. Again, many comparisons between his images and Link's can be made. For example, compare *Untitled (Oasis)* (2004)[67] with Link's well-known *Ghost Town* (NW 1345; see page 19).[68]

Given his influence on all of these artists, from noted railroad-subject photographers to art photographers, O. Winston Link stands as an important figure in the history and development of American photography. His work exemplifies the move away from "straight" or photojournalistic photography to photography allowing a vision created by the artist, rather than a document of an external "decisive moment." Given the adoption of digital photography, and the vast potential for manipulation of digital images, it seems likely this will continue to be an important direction in photographic art.

ON TO THE PHOTOGRAPHS

One Link image, *Hotshot Eastbound* (NW 1103; a photomontage; see page 22), is by far his most popular, and all but one of his most noted images (the exception is the daytime photo *Old Maude Bows to the Virginia Creeper* [NW 1230; see page 9]) are posed tableaux taken at night. However, as anyone who has reviewed the entire field of Link's N&W negatives knows, Link's Norfolk and Western project encompasses much more than the familiar images: There are a number of portraits, posed and unposed, of the people of the N&W and its service area. There are numerous more or less candid photos, many of them taken on the Abingdon Branch and many taken with a Rolleiflex. There are many variants of the famous images. Link's lifework also contains a number of excellent modernist images of steam locomotives, a portfolio almost certainly influenced by the early photography of Lucius Beebe. The

modernist style of photographs—most popular from 1910 to about 1940—was typified by photographers such as Walker Evans and Paul Strand; in the case of Beebe and Link, their photographs of this type were exemplified by clean, detached portraits of visually intriguing details of locomotives and, in Beebe's case, railroad passenger and freight cars, as well.[69] There are even a number of images, many of them taken in Nella (Husk), North Carolina, without a train in sight.

One of the purposes of this book is to give the interested reader a broader view of the entire range of Link's portfolio of the last years of the Norfolk and Western in steam, including excellent examples of both the keystone work and the photographs, such as the modernist images, that have not previously been published. Clearly, Link envisioned his project as an entity in and of itself. But the vast number of images available, enough to fill twenty books, means that the project's photographs will never be presented together in one publication. Representing the broad sweep of images found in the entire project, the selection of more than 180 photos presented in the plates that follow is divided into four categories: images of people, posed and unposed ("Railroaders"); images of locomotives ("Iron Horses"); portraits of the total railroad-influenced environment present in the Norfolk and Western's service area before the victory of the automobile and airplane ended passenger service on the line ("Side by Side"); and photographs depicting life in the N&W's service region and the communities served by the railroad ("In the 'Land of Plenty'"). A final set of images demonstrating how Link shot his photos and taped his sound recordings ("How It Was Done") precedes a technical notes section at the end of the book.

PLATES

In retrospect, O. Winston Link's photos reflect a theme of transition. In the case of documenting the transition from steam to diesel, this was intentional. But he also captured a workforce facing dramatic change, and a small-town way of life that was about to experience seismic shifts.

The following plates focus on Link's images of Norfolk and Western employees. The steam engine was a mechanical beast requiring servicing by hordes of workers: engineers, firemen, hostlers, and roundhouse and shop employees. Its demise would also eliminate most of these workers' jobs. Similarly, unmechanized maintenance-of-way procedures required section gangs to be assigned to small stretches of track. The mechanization of track maintenance, significant abandonments of tracks, the adoption of mechanized "speeders" and then automotive "hi-railers,"[70] and the introduction of welded rail for main lines would soon make section gangs obsolete. They were replaced by large track crews realizing economies of scale by using heavy equipment to conduct track maintenance and improvement across entire railroad systems.

During the 1950s, especially in remote rural areas such as the Norfolk and Western territory Link photographed, the local train station was still a gateway—the source of mail delivery to the community post office; a link to the telegraphic electronic communications network of the day (usually Western Union–provided); a source for express and small package (less than carload lot, or LCL) service in the days before ubiquitous UPS and FedEx services; and a source for passenger service, allowing anyone who could pay the fare to access a nationwide railroad passenger network. Presiding over all these community services was the station agent. As railroads transitioned from providing retail services to becoming carriers of bulk

freight, these local railroad offices closed, and agents' jobs disappeared. Exacerbating this trend was the move from telegraph- or telephone-transmitted train orders, written manually by agents and handed up to trains with order hoops, to orders provided directly by radio communications between train dispatchers and train crews or, on main lines, automatically through signals similar to road-transport traffic lights.

Train crews also saw major reductions. The end of passenger service eliminated the need for passenger train crews, although the coming of Amtrak in 1971 preserved some of these positions. After steam locomotives were scrapped, by about 1960, the position of fireman was gradually phased out. And the change from handling and switching single cars and even LCL shipments to bulk freight carriage such as railroads handle today (a transition spanning the 1950s through about 2000) also reduced the size of crews. A usual steam-era freight train crew was five men: the conductor, the boss of the train; a brakeman (sometimes called a flagman) at the rear and one (often called the head-end brakeman) at the front; an engineer; and a fireman. Today, most run-through freights have just an engineer and a conductor. The loss of jobs in operating crews has, therefore, been enormous. Intensifying this loss, in this case over the last eighty years or so, is the abandonment of most of the light density branch lines and many of the secondary main lines[71] in the United States, and the elimination of the caboose, which housed the conductor and brakemen, in favor of a new technology, the "FRED" (flashing rear-end device), by the mid-1980s. So, Link captured a railroad workforce that was, even in the 1950s, facing a shattering decline in employment.

The photos in this chapter document work on the Norfolk

and Western before these massive reductions dramatically reduced railroad employment. The workers featured here fall into six general classes of employees. Two of these groups, engine-service and train-service employees, actually ran the N&W's trains. In the day and time covered by Link's project, this was a male line of work, and all of these images feature male employees.

In the first group, the engineer held the highest engine-service position on a train, and the photos of the confident elder statesmen of the rails in plates 1, 2, 5, and 21 demonstrate this. Look, for example, at the way fireman Spradlin gazes admiringly at engineer Kitts in plate 5; this photo captures the relationship clearly.

The plates showing the second group, the train-service employees—conductors, brakemen, and like occupations[72]—also demonstrate the very masculine environment created by the all-male, all-white operating workforce of the day and place in question. Prominent in one of the photos (plate 36), and in many not selected for this book, are pinup girl posters that would not be present in today's work environment. Link captured these candid images as he saw them, preserving a time before yet another transition—the coming of equal opportunity to train crews, which now include women and minorities.

There are also a number of images of men in a third group of railroad employees, those who serviced locomotives: electricians, engine supplymen, locomotive lubricators (Link loved this type of image—he took many photos of men lubricating N&W steam engines), laborers, and roundhouse workers, or shopmen. Notice how many of the tasks these men performed were focused on the needs of the steam engine.

The fourth general group of workers featured are employees at stations, yards, and signal towers: yard clerks, agents—including the only woman in this chapter, station agent Gladys Harriger at White Top, Virginia (plate 24)—operators, and the iconic train caller ("usher") Buck Stewart of Roanoke, Virginia (plate 34).

Link's oeuvre is surprisingly deficient in images of a fifth group of N&W employees, the maintenance-of-way workers, including sectionmen. The only image selected from this set of railroad crafts is plate 32, showing two African Americans swinging spike mauls.

Finally, railroads had executives—another class of employee that, beyond president R. H. "Race Horse" Smith, Link rarely photographed. Plates 26, 27, and 41 show men in hats and ties, which, then as now (perhaps minus the hat today), marked railroad employees as "management."

PORTRAIT OF ENGINEER RICHARD GUTHREY. SHAFFERS CROSSING.
ROANOKE, VIRGINIA, JULY 28, 1955, NW 345

Always fascinated by the men who served the N&W, Link made many portraits
during his travels along the line. Here, engineer Richard Guthrey is posed before
a group of locomotives at Shaffers Crossing.

ENGINEER A. B. REYNOLDS WITH HIS LOCOMOTIVE, CLASS J #602.
WILLIAMSON, WEST VIRGINIA, DECEMBER 23, 1958, NW 2012

In late December 1958, Winston Link and his nephew, Leroy "Corky" Zider,
rode Trains #15 and #16, the west- and eastbound *Cavalier*, between Roanoke,
Virginia, and Williamson, West Virginia, to make sound recordings for one of
Link's *Sounds of Steam Railroading* albums.

It was in Williamson that Link photographed Arthur B. "Buddy" Reynolds,
one of the *Cavalier*'s regular engineers. Reynolds retired in 1959, after a
spotless fifty-three-year record with the railroad.

TRAINMAN WITH DRINKING WATER CAN. WEST JEFFERSON,
NORTH CAROLINA, OCTOBER 1957, NW 1463

While at a stop in West Jefferson, a crew member of Train #201 carries a
galvanized can to refill with fresh drinking water.

F. C. ARMENTROUT, YARD CLERK. WAYNESBORO, VIRGINIA,
MARCH 16, 1955, NW 5

Yard clerk F. C. Armentrout is seated in the Waynesboro station office.
The Norfolk and Western's standard-issue Seth Thomas clock is to his
right, regulating his nights. This image was made on Link's second trip to
Waynesboro, after an initial visit in January, with better lighting and the blessing
of the company (see plate 69 for a photograph made during his first visit).

ENGINEER J. W. KITTS AND FIREMAN
R. A. SPRADLIN WITH CLASS J #603.
WILLIAMSON, WEST VIRGINIA,
JANUARY 1, 1959. NW 2072

Link made his seventeenth trip to the Norfolk
and Western from mid-December 1958 to
early January 1959. The trip was primarily
to make sound recordings for his series of
albums, *Sounds of Steam Railroading*. Only
a few photos were taken, with Link using his
handheld Rolleiflex camera to document his
recordings. He always liked to photograph
railroad workers, and here are two whom he
found in Williamson.

MECHANIC INSPECTING THE VALVE
GEAR OF A CLASS J. ROANOKE,
VIRGINIA, AUGUST 1956. NW 1161

While recording the unique audio sounds
of a locomotive inspection, Link also
photographed a mechanic at the Roanoke
station. The sound made by tapping parts
with a small hammer could indicate hidden
defects that required attention. Link's
microphone can just barely be seen along
the right side of the frame.

During his first trip to Virginia specifically to photograph the N&W, in March 1955, Link concentrated on activities at the Waynesboro station and at the locomotive servicing facilities at Shaffers Crossing, west of downtown Roanoke. This is the close-up version of three photos Link made of J. W. Dalhouse cleaning the headlight of Class K-2a #127, often used on Trains #1 and #2 between Roanoke and Hagerstown, Maryland. In all of the photos in this series, Link emphasized how small the human service workers were in comparison to the monstrous size of their machines.

Mr. Dalhouse and his supervisor thought that having his photo taken would only take a few moments, but working with Link was an exacting process. It required about two hours. The supervisor was annoyed, but the resulting three photos have turned out to be among Link's best-known images.

Two N&W railroad workers stand proudly with the massive tools of
their craft. To the left is O. N. Carroll, a machinist who had been with
the railroad for thirty-four years when the photograph was taken. The
younger man is R. H. Carrier, an engine hostler, responsible for handling
locomotives and maintaining their fires and boiler water levels while in
the roundhouse area.

   Both men worked on the night shift, and Link recalled that machinist
Carroll had helped him while Link was photographing at the Bristol
roundhouse earlier that year. Link's lighting cables had become tangled in
the turntable, pulling down a number of large reflectors, and Carroll had
assisted Link in reconnecting many broken wires.

In stall #1 of the sixteen-stall Bristol roundhouse, Class A laborer
J. H. Pope hoses down Class K-1 #104, while Class M #382, the one
used most frequently on the Abingdon Branch, and an S-1a switcher
locomotive wait their turns. The Bristol roundhouse was small, and Link
benefited from the great cooperation of the foremen and workers there.

The control of a steam locomotive requires skill. When well handled, it
will perform safely and efficiently. Here, a fireman concentrates as he and
an unseen engineer wait on a Class Y-6 serving as a pusher on Blue
Ridge Grade.

Engineer Fitzhugh T. Nichols and brakeman J. M. "Skutch" Stevens
stand proudly before Class M #382, Link's favorite locomotive on the
Abingdon Branch.

PLATE 13 OPPOSITE

LUBRICATING WRISTPIN. BLUEFIELD. WEST VIRGINIA.
JUNE 20. 1955. NW 85

By using a wide-angle lens on his view camera, Link emphasized
the huge scale of steam locomotive driving wheels. Here, engine
supplyman Dominick Gerarbi is using a high-pressure grease gun
to quickly grease the crosshead on the main rod connecting the
piston to the seventy-inch drivers of Class E-2a (4-6-2) #563, built
in 1912 in the N&W's Roanoke Locomotive Shops.

    The Class E passenger locomotives were built between 1905
and 1914. In the 1920s, they were replaced in mainline service
by the heavier Class K locomotives. Many were scrapped during
the 1930s, with most of the rest of the class being retired shortly
after World War II. By the mid-1950s, only two remained, #563 and
#578. They were used in local passenger service on the Clinch
Valley line, between Bluefield and Norton, Virginia.

PLATE 14 RIGHT

A FULL SIX-MAN CREW OF THE SECOND PIGEON CREEK
SHIFTER STANDING IN FRONT OF THEIR LOCOMOTIVE Y-6B
#2190. SCIOTO DIVISION. WEST OF WILLIAMSON.
WEST VIRGINIA. MARCH 15. 1960. NW 2186

On March 15, 1960, almost the last day in the five-year cycle
of photographing the N&W's steam locomotives, Link made
this image that so well documents American working men that
advertising rights for its use were later acquired by OshKosh
B'gosh, a leading manufacturer of work clothing. Here, standing
by Class Y-6b #2190, is the train crew that operated the Second
Pigeon Creek Shifter, transporting coal hoppers to and from mines
in southwest West Virginia.

PLATE 15 OPPOSITE

ABINGDON BRANCH LOCOMOTIVE AND
TRAIN CREW, WEST JEFFERSON,
NORTH CAROLINA, JUNE 17, 1955, NW 159

On June 17, 1955, Link spent the day riding
the Abingdon Branch with his handheld
camera, capturing images of the crew at stops
throughout the day. In this image, taken from the
top of an adjoining freight car, he has gathered
the crew of the Class M next to their locomotive.

PLATE 16 RIGHT

LUBRICATING A CLASS J, BRISTOL
ROUNDHOUSE, BRISTOL, VIRGINIA,
OCTOBER 1, 1957, NW 1525

Locomotive maintenance was done along the
line at facilities like the Bristol roundhouse,
where skilled mechanical crews serviced the
powerful machines. Although steam locomotive
maintenance is inherently grimy and dangerous,
the N&W was known for both efficiency
and safety.

The scale of a locomotive is never more clearly
seen than when paired with a human form.
Steam locomotives required labor-intensive
maintenance. N&W employees were rightly proud
of the superior condition of company equipment
and the service it provided to customers.

The N&W continuously improved its facilities to
gain efficiency. It built "lubritoriums" at several
key service locations to more effectively inspect
and grease locomotives. Engine supplyman
J. O. Haden holds one of the tools that made
such efficiency possible, the Alemite grease gun,
which forced grease into locomotive fittings using
compressed air.

    Many African Americans worked for the
N&W at this time, often in physically demanding
jobs such as this one. Typically, there would be
no advancement from the position for which
they were hired, but J. O. Haden arrived at the
beginning of the civil rights movement and later
became a skilled machinist with the railroad.

PLATE 19 OPPOSITE

COMPLETING TENDER FILLING.
WEST JEFFERSON, NORTH CAROLINA,
JUNE 17, 1955, NW 158

Link climbed on top of a freight car on an
adjoining track to photograph fireman D. S.
"Nick" Nichols filling the tender of Class M
#429. In addition to burning approximately
ten tons of coal in the 110-mile round trip,
the locomotive required several thousand
gallons of water. There were four water
tanks on the Abingdon Branch: one at
Abingdon, Virginia; another about halfway
along the run at Creek Junction, Virginia;
one at Tuckerdale, North Carolina, which
appears to have been little used; and this
one at West Jefferson, which was used
every time the train arrived.

PLATE 20 RIGHT

SANDING CLASS K-1 #104, BRISTOL
ROUNDHOUSE, BRISTOL, VIRGINIA,
OCTOBER 17, 1955, NW 614

Engine supplyman T. A. "Andy" Smith
fills the sand dome mounted on top of
the boiler of Class K-1 #104. To improve
traction, the engineer released sand from
the dome through pipes, which placed it
onto the rails in front of the locomotive's
driving wheels.

PLATE 21 PREVIOUS SPREAD, LEFT

ENGINEER A. B. REYNOLDS. WELCH, WEST VIRGINIA, 1958, NW 1810

With the brick station at Welch behind him, A. B. Reynolds checks his pocket
watch while leaning on the open doorway of a baggage car. Emphasizing
timeliness and punctuality, the N&W required that its employees use only
railroad-approved watches.

PLATE 22 PREVIOUS SPREAD, RIGHT

CREW OF S-1A SWITCHER #243. ROANOKE, VIRGINIA, APRIL 17, 1955,
NW 41

Class S-1a #243 was serving as switcher at the Roanoke passenger station.
Here, fireman P. B. Brooks and engineer A. L. Crawford are passing the N&W
general office buildings west of the station. R. H. Smith, the president of the
N&W, had his office on the second floor of the building seen behind
the locomotive.

PLATE 23 LEFT

LOCOMOTIVE TAKING WATER. SHAFFERS CROSSING, ROANOKE,
VIRGINIA, MARCH 19, 1955, NW 14

Roanoke was the hub of operations on the Norfolk and Western. The large
locomotive service facility located at Shaffers Crossing supported the yard
and locomotive maintenance shop there. Here, water fills the tender of a 0-8-0
locomotive, one of many serviced that day.

PLATE 24 OPPOSITE

GLADYS HARRIGER, AGENT AT THE WHITE TOP STATION. WHITE TOP,
VIRGINIA, OCTOBER 17, 1955, NW 660

Gladys Harriger was one of only four female station agents on the N&W in
1955. She kept the station tidy, handled waybills for any freight or express
that might be dropped off there, and filled the hours between Train #201,
southbound, and Train #202, northbound, by making quilts. The southbound
train was due in at 9:34 A.M., and the northbound train was expected at
1:06 P.M., but handling freight on the mixed train took precedence, so the train
might arrive considerably later. Mrs. Harriger has raised her chair by fitting the
legs with insulators used on telegraph poles, which also allows the chair to
glide across the rough floor.

Gladys Harriger was famous in the area for having held Train #202 at
White Top for three hours during a deep snowfall on March 5, 1942, so that
a critically ill woman having a difficult labor could be brought to the train and
rushed to a hospital in Abingdon. Once the woman was safely on board, the
train made the trip nonstop. To honor the railroad's good service, the child was
named Richard Norwest Weaver.

In 1955 the hard work of baggage handling was done by hand. Parcels were loaded onto carts and sent to their destination. With an audience of many, two men get the work done.

Thomas Pucket served as section foreman for the N&W for forty-five years and two months. Proudly dressed in a suit like those that managers wore, he stands at the scissor gate of a passenger car traveling near Cedar Bluff.

PLATE 27 LEFT

J. W. ELLIS, TWENTY-SIX YEARS WITH THE
NORFOLK AND WESTERN. BLUEFIELD,
WEST VIRGINIA, OCTOBER 6, 1955,
NW 444

J. W. Ellis, who worked for the N&W for twenty-
six years, stands before Class G-1 #7 as it's
moved to its final home in a Bluefield park.
Moving this engine captured the attention of the
city, which formed an impromptu parade as the
#7 wound through the streets of Bluefield.

PLATE 28 OPPOSITE

SWITCH TOWER OPERATOR MILLER
RUTH IN HAGER TOWER. HAGERSTOWN,
MARYLAND, JANUARY 27, 1957, NW 1383

Miller Ruth was one of the principal operators of
the Hager interlocking tower. Link recalled that
Ruth was proud of his job and always wore a tie
to work, in part to distinguish himself from the
switchmen who had to work outside in the yards
during all kinds of weather.

PLATE 29 PREVIOUS SPREAD, LEFT

GEORGE BEAGHAN IN THE STATION. SHENANDOAH
JUNCTION, WEST VIRGINIA, JULY 28, 1956. NW 1075

All of the fittings of a small railroad station are here: the Railway
Express Agency strongbox for high-value shipments, a pair of extra
flags to be mounted on the locomotive, red and white kerosene
signal lanterns, a battered typewriter, and a filing cabinet. Link loved
the appliances and apparatus of the railroad, particularly because so
much of it was old, and he liked to photograph railroad workers set
in this dusty, slightly shabby environment, where there was real work
to be done.

PLATE 30 PREVIOUS SPREAD, RIGHT

INTERIOR OF HAGER TOWER. HAGERSTOWN, MARYLAND,
MARCH 18, 1956. NW 805

The Hager interlocking tower was manned twenty-four hours a day
by Pennsylvania Railroad employees, who controlled switches and
signals covering the three railroads that intersected there: the N&W,
the Pennsylvania, and the Western Maryland. Such interlocking
towers could control switches and signals many hundreds of
feet away and direct rail traffic safely through complex junctions.
Today, such work is controlled by central dispatchers, who may be
hundreds of miles away. Hager Tower is no longer standing.

PLATE 31 LEFT

STATION AGENT'S DESK THROUGH THE STATION AGENT'S
WINDOW. LURAY, VIRGINIA, MARCH 20, 1956. NW 921

It's a quiet night in Luray, and through the cracked window of the
station agent's quarters, time is standing still. Feet propped up on a
tidy desk, the station agent waits for something to happen.

PLATE 32 OPPOSITE

MAINTENANCE-OF-WAY WORKERS DRIVING SPIKES.
BLUEFIELD, WEST VIRGINIA, OCTOBER 6, 1955. NW 443

In October 1955, the N&W moved Class G-1 #7 to a park in
Bluefield. Over the course of several days, Link captured the process
of moving this locomotive from track to trailer to its final home in the
park. Showing the hard work of driving spikes, in this image Link
captured the symmetry and strength of a maintenance-of-way crew
as they lay track for the #7.

PLATE 33 PREVIOUS SPREAD, LEFT

HANDING UP ORDERS. HAGERSTOWN, MARYLAND,

JANUARY 28, 1957, NW 1331

All aspects of this time-honored scene have vanished from the modern American railroad: the steam locomotive, the mechanical interlocking tower, and the passing of train orders to the engineer, using an order fork. The time is about 1 A.M., in January 1957. Class K-2a #127 is moving from the Pennsylvania Railroad roundhouse in Hagerstown, and will be picking up Train #1, southbound, for the rest of its run from New York City to Roanoke, Virginia. Night switch tower operator Albert Blair waits to hand up train movement orders to the engineer, using the order fork. Train orders were tightly folded and held between the uprights of the fork by lightweight string. The tower operator could pass them up to the engineer of a moving train, who would grab them on the fly.

PLATE 34 PREVIOUS SPREAD, RIGHT

BUCK STEWART CALLING TRAINS, ROANOKE STATION. ROANOKE,

VIRGINIA, AUGUST 5, 1956, NW 1118

Harry T. "Buck" Stewart worked for the railroad for decades. Link recalled that Stewart had earlier been employed on a maintenance-of-way crew, where he had been injured, and was subsequently reassigned to the less strenuous task of announcing the trains at the N&W's modern Roanoke passenger station. Link described Stewart as having "an inimitable way of calling trains in a voice which was a combination of gravel and southern drawl."

The hard surfaces of the building produced so many echoes that Stewart had learned to pace his announcements slowly enough so that the name of every destination town he called could be clearly understood. In this photo, he is seen standing in the passenger concourse, which extended from the present station out over the tracks below. This was demolished in 1992 to permit higher freight loads to pass through the city.

PLATE 35 LEFT

M. V. YATES PUFFING ON HIS PIPE. ABINGDON BRANCH,

JUNE 18, 1955, NW 264

Always interested in the people who served the N&W, Link made many portraits of the crews with whom he rode. Riding the Abingdon Branch on June 18, 1955, Link photographed M. V. Yates, smoking his pipe and wearing a pair of N&W overalls.

PLATE 36 OPPOSITE

EARL CARPER TYING HIS SHOE. DAMASCUS, VIRGINIA,

JUNE 18, 1955, NW 284

Earl Carper is tying his shoe against an open trunk. The pinup photo in the lid of his trunk was common in the all-male railroad environment of that era.

PLATE 37 OPPOSITE
BRAKEMAN OF THE SECOND PIGEON CREEK SHIFTER ON
CABOOSE. KERMIT, WEST VIRGINIA, MARCH 16, 1960,
NW 2193

In Kermit, a brakeman poses on a caboose, separated from the
photographer by several chains, creating a visual Y.

PLATE 38 RIGHT
UPPER FIGURE OF BRAKEMAN IN FRONT OF Y-6B #2179.
BLUE RIDGE, VIRGINIA, JUNE 1958, NW 1858

Sporting a nonstandard cap, a brakeman stands on the platform of
his caboose with pusher locomotive Y-6b #2179 behind him. Link
photographed the pusher on Blue Ridge Grade extensively from
the caboose, a perspective not often seen in railroad photography.

PLATE 39 OVERLEAF, LEFT
SKUTCH STEVENS SMOKES A CIGARETTE IN PASSENGER
CAR. ABINGDON BRANCH, JUNE 17, 1955, NW 190A

The Abingdon Branch was a small and less-traveled branch line
of the N&W, with limited service that operated only during the day.
Link noticed the informal camaraderie between the crew and the
passengers here. Inside the only passenger car on the Abingdon
Branch mixed train, Skutch Stevens posed for this portrait while
enjoying a smoke.

PLATE 40 OVERLEAF, RIGHT
CHECKING THE LEVEL OF WATER IN THE TENDER OF
S-1A #243. ROANOKE, VIRGINIA, AUGUST 1956, NW 1166

While inspecting their locomotive, crew members manually check
the tender water level. As shown here on the right, the vertical pipe
sprays water, indicating the level of water remaining in the tender.
This S-1a switcher served the Roanoke terminal. In the distance,
the railroad's majestic Hotel Roanoke overlooks the station.

PLATE 41 LEFT

W. D. "BILL" EMMONS, BRISTOL ROUNDHOUSE FOREMAN.
BRISTOL ROUNDHOUSE, BRISTOL, VIRGINIA,
NOVEMBER 1, 1957, NW 1578

Foreman Bill Emmons stands out from the rest of the roundhouse crew in a coat and tie, dress often worn by managers. Southern Railway diesel locomotives peek over Emmons's shoulder as he poses in front of the water tank in the Bristol yard.

PLATE 42 OPPOSITE

THE HONEY HOLE, BOAZ SIDING ON BLUE RIDGE GRADE.
VINTON, VIRGINIA, SEPTEMBER 6, 1958, NW 1977

Blue Ridge Grade, just a few miles east of Roanoke, is a 1.2 percent grade, stretching for eight and a half miles. Blue Ridge Grade was the last ascending grade facing eastbound coal before the long descent to the Tidewater region. The N&W stationed Class Y-6 locomotives at Boaz Siding, at the foot of Blue Ridge Grade, to assist heavy coal and merchandise freights eastbound. The location where the pusher crew waited was pleasant, with a little table under a willow tree by a stream. The engine crews kept it tidy, but because there were no sanitary facilities there, the place earned the ironic nickname the "Honey Hole."

For one of his most theatrical images, Link carefully set the scene. To the left, the engineer and fireman finish their coffee as their locomotive steams quietly behind them, and the caboose of the next train to be pushed over the grade rolls slowly to a stop at the right. Link even provided a special lantern on the caboose. It was wired with a flashbulb and was handed up to the brakeman as the caboose passed the pusher locomotive's tender. This was a photograph Link particularly enjoyed because of the way in which the willow tree draped over the scene.

Link picked the Norfolk and Western as a subject largely because it was the last major steam-operated railroad in the United States. The photos in this chapter document the major types of locomotives on which Link liked to focus his lens.

These fell into six major classes. Link's images of passenger trains and locomotives highlighted two types of locomotives: Norfolk and Western classes J and K. The Class J, considered by many the finest steam passenger locomotive ever produced in the United States, was one of the four most advanced types of N&W steam locomotives (the others were classes A, Y-6, and S-1).[73] The Class J was a 4-8-4 high-speed passenger locomotive intended for mainline service, built by the N&W itself during the years 1941 to 1950.[74] A single Class J, #611, survives of the fourteen produced (they were numbered 600 to 613). The 611 is held at the Virginia Museum of Transportation in Roanoke, very close to the O. Winston Link Museum.[75]

The Class J replaced the Class K 4-8-2 Mountain-type passenger engines on mainline passenger trains during the 1940s. The newer Class Ks on the roster (K-2 and K-2a) were then modified and streamlined to resemble the Class Js. During Link's Norfolk and Western project, he often photographed Class Ks leading passenger trains on one of his favorite sections of the railway, the Shenandoah Valley line. All of the 100-series Class K Mountain-type passenger locomotives, numbered 100 to 137, were scrapped in the late 1950s. They had been built by the N&W, and by commercial locomotive manufacturers Brooks and Baldwin, in 1916, 1917, 1919, and 1923.

On small branch lines and short lines throughout the United States, mixed trains offered both passenger and freight service.

Slow and inconvenient, they crumpled in the face of automotive competition. By the 1950s, they lingered on only in the most isolated corners of the country. One such corner—literally the spot where Virginia, Tennessee, and North Carolina meet—was the province of the Abingdon Branch mixed train, commonly known as the "Virginia Creeper" (so called by people of the area because of its slow schedule; officially they were trains 201 and 202). During Link's Norfolk and Western project, this train was pulled by a stable of elderly and unusual Class M 4-8-0 locomotives, a type near and dear to the photographer's heart. The Class M was originally very large, with roster numbers 375 to 499 (M), 1000 to 1099 (M-1), 1100 to 1149 (M-2), and 1150 to 1160 (M-2a, b, c). During Link's time photographing the Abingdon Branch, the Class Ms used there were usually numbers 382, 396, and 429.[76] All of these are from the oldest group of Class Ms, built in 1906 and 1907. Class M #433 survives and is on display in Abingdon, Virginia, at the beginning of the Virginia Creeper Trail, and Class M #475 may be seen in operation on the Strasburg Rail Road.[77]

The freight locomotives that caught Link's eye, and camera, were arguably the two most well-developed steam freight locomotives ever constructed in the United States. Class A 2-6-6-4 locomotives, numbered 1200 through 1242, were constructed by the Norfolk and Western from 1936 to 1950. They were simple articulated locomotives intended for time (fast) freight service. They could also haul passenger trains, and often did during the dire early days of World War II. Class A #1218 survives today next to the Class J #611 at the Virginia Museum of Transportation. Complementing the Class A on N&W freights were the Class Y-6, Y-6a, and Y-6b 2-8-8-2 locomotives, numbers 2120 to 2200, built by the N&W

from 1936 to 1952. The Class Y-6 was a true Mallet compound locomotive, a modern heavy freight locomotive often used to haul coal trains. One Class Y-6a survives, at the St. Louis Museum of Transportation in Missouri.

Finally, Link often photographed the Norfolk and Western's most modern steam switching locomotives, the S-1 and S-1a 0-8-0. (S-1a's were numbered 200 to 244 and were built by the N&W during 1951 to 1953; S-1s were numbered 255 to 284, but unlike the other three modern N&W locomotive types, the S-1 was not designed by the N&W—they were built by Baldwin for the Chesapeake & Ohio in 1948, and were purchased by the N&W in 1950; some S-1a's were renumbered 290 to 295 in 1960.) All of the S-1 and S-1a locomotives were scrapped.

This is the chapter in the book with the fewest number of plates. The brevity is due to the fact that Link, as he stated in his original letter to the Norfolk and Western's management, intended to show an N&W employee in every photograph he took as part of the project—so photos centered on locomotives are relatively scarce. Some of the views in this chapter show employees, but they are dwarfed by their massive steel charges.

Plates 43 and 45 to 48 present images of the type that made Link famous: dramatic night photographs. These images, of course, are of locomotives, including classes Y-6, J, K, and S-1a.

Plates 49, 53, 58, and 66 present a selection of high-modern, detail photos of steam power. Plates 59, 60, 62, and 63 (daytime images of one of Link's favorite photo locations, Montgomery Tunnel near Christiansburg, Virginia), show engines at full steam and speed. This series of images also includes a similar view at Pembroke Tunnel in Virginia.

Closing this chapter is an image of a double-headed Virginia Creeper behind two of the most primitive locomotives Link regularly photographed, Class Ms, and a rare Link night view of the spoilers who ended the steam era on the N&W: two fairly new GP-9 diesels standing next to a now-useless water tank at Shaffers Crossing, Roanoke, Virginia, in March 1960.

CLASS Y-6B IN THE WASH BAY AT BLUEFIELD. BLUEFIELD,
WEST VIRGINIA, JULY 27, 1955, NW 343

Up until the very end of steam power on the N&W, all locomotives received a
wash as part of their maintenance and service. A high-pressure blast of steam
and hot water, mixed with a little kerosene, washed away the dirt. The hot boiler
of this locomotive speeds the drying process in a cloud of steam, which Link has
emphasized by putting lights behind the subject as well as in front of it.

CLASS Y-6A ENGINE #2159 LOOKING THROUGH ROUNDHOUSE DOOR.
BRISTOL ROUNDHOUSE, BRISTOL, VIRGINIA, OCTOBER 1, 1957,
NW 1531

Being readied for a time freight run back to Roanoke, Class Y-6a is seen through
a partially closed door at the Bristol roundhouse.

CLASS J #605 ENTERS THE WASH BAY. SHAFFERS CROSSING,
ROANOKE, VIRGINIA, MARCH 19, 1955, NW 12

After Link's initial few test photos at Waynesboro, Virginia, in January 1955, the
huge Shaffers Crossing locomotive servicing facility west of downtown Roanoke
was the first site of his N&W photos, made in March 1955. Here, Class J #605
glides into position for a high-pressure wash of water, steam, and kerosene,
which will leave it glistening. Link liked to joke that "the dirt on N&W engines is
a deposit of diesel soot thrown off by C&O and Virginian locomotives that run
parallel to the N&W in many places."

CLASS K-1 #104 TAKING ON WATER. BRISTOL ROUNDHOUSE, BRISTOL,
VIRGINIA, OCTOBER 17, 1955, NW 611

Bristol was the southwestern terminus for the N&W. The roundhouse there
was small and generally quiet. Class J locomotives pulling passenger trains
westbound were serviced there after handing their trains to the diesels of the
Southern Railway. The three Class M locomotives used on the Abingdon Branch
were kept there, as was Class K-1 #104, built in the N&W's Roanoke Shops
in 1916 for passenger service, but now finishing its days moving local freight.
Because Link was in the area on a number of occasions to photograph the
Abingdon Branch, he would often spend his evenings making photos at the
Bristol roundhouse.

Here, locomotive #104 has been moved from its stall and is taking on coal
and water, while another shop man lubricates its running gear.

PLATE 47 OPPOSITE

CLASS S-1A #203, BLUEFIELD, WEST VIRGINIA,
JULY 27, 1955, NW 338

Engineer Dan Annel and turntable operator Arno
Cundiff release the steam from a cylinder cock on
S-1a #203 in Bluefield.

PLATE 48 RIGHT

CLASS S-1A #201 ON THE TURNTABLE,
SHAFFERS CROSSING, ROANOKE, VIRGINIA,
APRIL 16, 1955, NW 29

On this April night in 1955, S-1a #201 is posed on the
turntable at Shaffers Crossing in Roanoke. Link's flash
adds a glow to an otherwise very dark scene.

PLATE 49 OVERLEAF, LEFT

HEADLIGHT OF CLASS Y-6A #2159, BRISTOL,
VIRGINIA, OCTOBER 1, 1957, NW 1536

The Bristol roundhouse provided Link with a ready
field of willing subjects. Getting close to, on, and
around the locomotives gave him the opportunity
to explore all parts of the machines that served the
railroad. Behind its utilitarian features shines the
headlight of Class Y-6a #2159.

PLATE 50 OVERLEAF, RIGHT

CLASS Y-6A AT SHAFFERS CROSSING,
ROANOKE, VIRGINIA, JANUARY 4, 1958,
NW 1671

Link has captured the forward right side of a Class
Y-6a cloaked in a cloud of steam. The form of
this locomotive follows its function: Each feature
contributes to its ability to move freight. The N&W
refined the design of its locomotives to include the
most modern and efficient features available.

PLATE 51 PREVIOUS SPREAD, LEFT

CLASS K-1 #114 ON THE TURNTABLE, BRISTOL
ROUNDHOUSE, BRISTOL, VIRGINIA, NOVEMBER 1, 1957,
NW 1574

Turntables were required to reverse the direction of locomotives
and gain access to shop tracks in the roundhouse, and were the
hub of most steam locomotive service facilities. In this image,
Class K-1 #114 rides the Bristol turntable.

PLATE 52 PREVIOUS SPREAD, RIGHT

CLASS J IN ROUNDHOUSE, BRISTOL ROUNDHOUSE,
BRISTOL, VIRGINIA, OCTOBER 1, 1957, NW 1530

An unknown Class J locomotive is at rest in the Bristol roundhouse.
Class J locomotives used to deliver passenger trains to the
Southern Railway at Bristol were serviced there.

PLATE 53 OPPOSITE

MAIN DRIVING PIN AND ROLLER BEARING, CONNECTING
RODS OF A CLASS J, BRISTOL, VIRGINIA, OCTOBER 1, 1957,
NW 1535

The Norfolk and Western designed and operated arguably the
finest modern steam locomotives. Link was interested in both the
machines and the people who ran them. This design-centric image
focuses on the details of the valve gear and connecting rods of a
Class J locomotive.

PLATE 54 RIGHT

CLASS J #602 STARTS A TRAIN, WYTHEVILLE, VIRGINIA,
1957, NW 1713

Using his handheld Rolleiflex camera, Link made a series of images
of Class J #602 arriving at and then departing the Wytheville
station. Here, the locomotive's exhaust condenses in the cold air as
the crew starts its train westbound.

PLATE 55 LEFT

CLASS Y-6B #2190. NEAR KERMIT. WEST VIRGINIA.
MARCH 15, 1960. NW 2182

In 1960, steam power on the Norfolk and Western Railway was found only in the coal-mining districts of southern West Virginia. On March 15, 1960, almost the last day of his documentation of steam on the N&W, Link took his tape recorder on the Second Pigeon Creek Shifter, a train that delivered empty hopper cars to various mines and picked up cars that had been loaded with coal. He also made documentary photos like this one using his medium-format Rolleiflex camera. Y-6b #2190 was the last N&W steam locomotive in revenue service when all fires were dropped in early May 1960.

PLATE 56 OPPOSITE

SWITCHER PUSHING A CABOOSE THROUGH ROANOKE.
ROANOKE, VIRGINIA, DECEMBER 31, 1958, NW 2054

As the junction of the north-to-south and east-to-west lines of the N&W, Roanoke was always a busy area. This S-1a switcher is moving through Roanoke and past one of several general office buildings on its way to Shaffers Crossing.

PLATE 57 OVERLEAF, LEFT

CLASS Y-5 #2118. WILLIAMSTON, WEST VIRGINIA,
MARCH 14, 1960, NW 2234

Taken while recording a whistle sequence, this is one of the last images made during Link's Norfolk and Western project.

PLATE 58 OVERLEAF, RIGHT

CLASS Y-6A BUILDER'S PLATE. SHAFFERS CROSSING. ROANOKE.
VIRGINIA, JANUARY 4, 1958. NW 1670

Interested in every part of the railroad, Link focused his view camera upward to capture a modernist view of the builder's plate on a Class Y-6a. The builder's plate provided the identification number and manufacturing information for the locomotive.

PLATE 59 PREVIOUS SPREAD, LEFT

EMPTY COAL CARS MOVING WEST AT MONTGOMERY
TUNNEL, NEAR CHRISTIANSBURG, VIRGINIA,
DECEMBER 20, 1955, NW 741

After making several shots at this location (see plate 108), Link
returned to Montgomery Tunnel to take photographs in the
daylight. He liked the location because the westbound trains were
moving upgrade, so the locomotives were working hard. The
smoke and steam exhaust were trapped inside the tunnel, so the
locomotives usually came out in a cloud of vapor, which made for
spectacular photos. The tunnel was also at the base of a deep cut,
so Link worked at the top to capture a dramatic angle, looking down
at the locomotives as they left the tunnel.

PLATE 60 PREVIOUS SPREAD, RIGHT

CLASS J AT MONTGOMERY TUNNEL, NEAR
CHRISTIANSBURG, VIRGINIA, DECEMBER 20, 1955,
NW 124K

A Class J, pulling the *Powhatan Arrow*, exits Montgomery Tunnel
east of Christiansburg. The train provided first-class service from
Norfolk, Virginia, to Cincinnati, Ohio.

PLATE 61 OPPOSITE

PEMBROKE TUNNEL, PEMBROKE, VIRGINIA,
AUGUST 10, 1956, NW 1135

Link captured Class Y-6 #2145 coming out of the tunnel. He took
several photos in this location but printed none for exhibition during
his lifetime. The neutral tone of the background, foreground, and
locomotive does not conceal the harsh terrain along the N&W line, a
stark contrast to the more edited versions of the landscape visible in
his night images.

PLATE 62 RIGHT

TIME FREIGHT MOVING WEST AT MONTGOMERY TUNNEL,
NEAR CHRISTIANSBURG, VIRGINIA, DECEMBER 20, 1955,
NW 745

A time freight train is seen moving west at Montgomery Tunnel. This
view looks west with the eastbound signal heads in the foreground.
The Class Y-6 has exited the tunnel and will soon reach the summit
at Christiansburg.

PLATE 67 OPPOSITE

LEAVING GREEN COVE. GREEN COVE, VIRGINIA,
OCTOBER 23, 1956, NW 1241

With the throttles barely cracked and the locomotives all but
blowing smoke rings, double-headed Train #201, southbound,
leaves Green Cove. The train will have to pick up speed, however,
to take on the 3 percent grade for the next few miles to White Top.
The second locomotive, Class M #396, was normally held in reserve
at the roundhouse in Bristol, and used infrequently on the run.

PLATE 68 RIGHT

SERVICING EMD DIESEL-ELECTRICS. SHAFFERS CROSSING,
ROANOKE, VIRGINIA, MARCH 1960, NW 120C

In one of the few night color photographs he made, Link has
stopped time on a cold March night. As the N&W transitioned from
steam to diesel, the method for servicing locomotives changed. No
longer are water towers needed, unless to create steam heat for
passenger cars. No longer are the mundane tasks of a busy service
yard required. That hush is compounded by the quiet of the snow
on the ground.

American railroad-subject photography was undergoing a transition of its own. Beginning in the late 1940s, a movement started among the young photographers featured in *Railroad* and *Trains* magazines. These men—they were all men—included Philip R. Hastings, Richard Steinheimer, and Jim Shaughnessy. Their innovation, arguably initiated by Charles Clegg in images featured in the 1947 book *Mixed Train Daily*,[78] by Lucius Beebe, was to back away from the "smoking wedge" shot (a three-quarter view of an approaching train in motion, focused on the locomotive, with it preferably producing noticeable smoke in the image) popularized by Beebe, to take on a broader view of the railroad environment. Beyond Clegg, who hovered under the shadow of his working partner, Beebe, the innovator leading the development of this type of railroad-subject photograph was Hastings. Under the editorship of David P. Morgan at *Trains*, and following Hastings's lead, these photographers expanded their work from the traditional roster (posed locomotive portrait photograph) and action scenes that preceded them into a holistic view of the American railroad environment.[79]

These photographers did not intend to create art: Their aim, as much as it was articulated, was to document the richness of American railroading as it faced major changes, exemplified by the end of railroad steam and the decline of the local, staffed railroad station. Despite their documentarian goals, Hastings, Steinheimer, and Shaughnessy created a number of images with great artistic worth; Steinheimer and Shaughnessy have recently garnered recognition as notable American photographers.

Throughout the early and mid-1950s, Hastings continued to lead this movement in American railroad-subject photography—a because it sought to go beyond views of the locomotive to record the entire scene of American railroading. Hastings's influence during the 1950s was largely a result of his notable series of articles— "In Search of Steam," "Smoke Over the Prairies," and "Steam in Indian Summer"—done in collaboration with Morgan during the period from 1954 to 1958 and featured in *Trains*. The articles, taken together, provide important documentation of the end of steam on American and Canadian railroads.

Link was in correspondence with, and was featured in, *Trains* during this period, and his photography clearly shows the influence of Hastings and Morgan. In his manifesto letter to the Norfolk and Western, already cited, he mentioned making "well-planned night photographs . . . showing the railroad at work as the passenger sleeps" and including "an employee in every picture." But, almost immediately, Link joined Hastings in broadening his focus to include the entire scene of steam railroading as it was practiced on the N&W after World War II.

The plates in this chapter show a selection of Link's views of the railroading environment along the Norfolk and Western. It begins with plate 69, Link's first N&W image, *Train #2 Arrives at the Waynesboro Station* (NW 1; taken January 21, 1955), a Hastings-like night photo showing a streamlined Class K passing through the unique, two-level Waynesboro, Virginia, depot as the agent hands up orders to the engine crew.

Plates 70 to 81 continue the series of images taken at night or in darkness, as N&W steam locomotives thunder across bridges or past waiting passengers, train order signals, and railroad signal towers, where railroad lines cross or join.

Several of the photos place switch lamps or lanterns in the foreground to great artistic effect, and a number of them feature the characteristic lines of the pre–Norfolk and Western frame depots (circa the late 1860s) located at places such as Rural Retreat and Max Meadows, as well as at many locations on the N&W in Virginia not photographed by Link. One of the nighttime images in this series (plate 76) is a technical tour de force: a Class Y-6 taken inside a tunnel.

A modernist view of crossing gates in Roanoke, Virginia (plate 82), provides a transition to a series of images of 1950s railroading on the Norfolk and Western in daylight. Link's artistry is evident in images of locomotives starting in clouds of steam, and posed by boxcars with fascinating markings (THE GRAND CANYON LINE), ancient wooden tugboats, and oil storage tanks. Steam-drawn trains cross high bridges, meet at junctions, and pass trackside signs, mines, and boys at a station. A locomotive during the very last days of steam on the N&W seems threatened by sword-like icicles (plate 92). In another favorite Link image, a pusher locomotive (used to provide extra power to assist trains uphill) looms through an open caboose door, seemingly about to crush the diminutive item of rolling stock[80] in front of it (plate 93). This series concludes with three images: a modernist view of signs at a tunnel mouth, and a Class A at a water tank, being followed by its fatal enemy, a new Norfolk

Many of the images in this daytime series are of the Virginia Creeper (plates 86, 90, 97, 98, and 101 to 106)—the mixed train serving the N&W Abingdon Branch that ran from Abingdon, Virginia, to West Jefferson, North Carolina (and, in earlier years, on to Todd, or Elkland, North Carolina). This was Link's favorite part of the N&W system, and fortunately much of it has been preserved for the public to enjoy as the Virginia Creeper Trail, which runs thirty-four miles from Abingdon to White Top, Virginia. A striking and little-known, image shows the Virginia Creeper posed beside a modern bus (plate 90). The contrast between the sooty Class M and the gleaming motor coach is stark, and prophetic. Plate 101 shows a different view of the Green Cove, Virginia, station, familiar from the famous *Old Maude Bows to the Virginia Creeper* (see page 9)—a look at the structure from the fireman's side of an Abingdon-bound Class M.

This chapter closes with another prophetic image: a view from the top of the cab of an old Class M, looking out of place on trackage along the N&W main line running through Abingdon to Bristol, Virginia, passing a Class Y-6a that looks very modern in comparison. Just a few years after this 1955 image was taken, all N&W steam would be gone.

PLATE 69 LEFT

TRAIN #2 ARRIVES AT THE WAYNESBORO
STATION. WAYNESBORO, VIRGINIA,
JANUARY 21, 1955. NW 1

This is Link's first photo of the steam
locomotives of the Norfolk and Western Railway.
It was created on January 21, 1955, as the
N&W's Train #2, northbound from Roanoke to
Hagerstown, Maryland, and on to New York
City, arrived in Waynesboro. From the very
first photo, Link demonstrated his interest in
making a record of both steam locomotives and
the environment in which they operated, and
that included the railroad's buildings. He was
particularly interested in recording the human
activities that were part of running the railroad.
Here, station agent Troy Humphries uses a
message fork to hand up train orders to the
engineer of Class K-2a #130 as it slows
to a stop.

The N&W management was delighted with
the photo, except that the steam escaping from
the safety valve indicated that the boiler pressure
was too high and therefore that coal was being
wasted. Link was asked by the railroad not to
take photos of locomotives that were making
black smoke or had the safety valves open. He
tried to comply, but it was not always possible.

PLATE 70 OPPOSITE

FREIGHT #88 NORTH. NATURAL BRIDGE
STATION, VIRGINIA, MARCH 28, 1956.
NW 871

The approach into the Natural Bridge station was
spectacular, as the N&W's tracks first passed
over a long bridge crossing the James River,
with another truss span immediately onshore,
crossing over the Chesapeake and Ohio Railway.
The station platform, where four boys watch a
passing merchandise train, began immediately
north of the bridge.

MAX MEADOWS STATION AT DUSK.
MAX MEADOWS, VIRGINIA,
DECEMBER 1957, NW 102K

Photographing in color at night was one
more technical obstacle that Link overcame
during the N&W project. Obtaining a
balanced exposure was especially difficult.
This striking low-angle view of the Max
Meadows station is one of the few night
color images Link ever made.

THE BIRMINGHAM SPECIAL. EAST
AT MAX MEADOWS. MAX MEADOWS,
VIRGINIA, DECEMBER 22, 1957,
NW 1618

Train #18, the *Birmingham Special*, with
Class J #604 at the head, was eastbound
from Birmingham, Alabama, to New York
City. The train didn't stop in Max Meadows,
but was scheduled to pass through at
4:28 A.M. Early in the morning of
December 22, 1957, Link was ready to
take the photo—as all steam power on
the N&W's passenger service line from
Bristol to Roanoke, Virginia, was due to
be terminated on January 1, 1958. Link
spent several days at Max Meadows,
taking photos from a few inches above the
ground, as shown here, to photographing
the passing locomotives from a signal
bridge high above the tracks.

PLATE 73 PREVIOUS SPREAD, LEFT

TRAIN #88 EAST AT MAX MEADOWS. MAX MEADOWS, VIRGINIA,
DECEMBER 22, 1957, NW 1621

Train #88 passes by, heading east, as Max Meadows residents Minnie Tate,
Terry Friend, and Kerry Friend wave to the crew on the caboose platform. Link
has placed his lights out of sight, to the left of the frame, but the powerful
flashbulbs create some fog in the dark night.

PLATE 74 PREVIOUS SPREAD, RIGHT

TRAIN #17, THE BIRMINGHAM SPECIAL, ARRIVING AT RURAL RETREAT.
RURAL RETREAT, VIRGINIA, DECEMBER 26, 1957, NW 1628

Train #17 arrives at Rural Retreat, while Dallas Newman and his daughter Mary
Elizabeth wait on the platform.

PLATE 75 LEFT

THE LONE STAR SHIFTER GETS UNDER WAY. CLOVERDALE, VIRGINIA,
FEBRUARY 8, 1957, NW 1359

Link loved big objects in the foreground of his photos, which helped emphasize
their deep space. He was so attracted to the idea of having a semaphore
signal in the foreground of one of his images that he constructed a camera
platform on the roof of the N&W station in Cloverdale. It's a testament to his
vision that he could imagine just how this photo would look, when it existed
for only the fraction of a second that the flashbulbs burned. On this evening in
February 1957, a cold rain was falling as the Lone Star Shifter thundered past
the Cloverdale station, bound for Roanoke on the main line of the Shenandoah
Division. It had picked up a number of cars of cement at the Lone Star Cement
Corporation. The company, served by an 8.8-mile spur line branching from
Cloverdale, continues to ship large quantities of cement by rail today.

PLATE 76 OPPOSITE

PIGEON CREEK SHIFTER INSIDE MINGO TUNNEL. WILLIAMSON,
WEST VIRGINIA, MARCH 1960, NW 123C

In the last days of the N&W project, Link was determined to capture a few more
images and recordings before all steam locomotives were retired. Class Y-6
#2136 flashes past with the Pigeon Creek Shifter inside Mingo Tunnel. He has
captured the power and energy of a Y-6 in a confined space, in this beautiful
image with perfectly balanced color.

PLATE 77 LEFT

96 NORTH, LURAY CROSSING, LURAY, VIRGINIA,
MARCH 22, 1956, NW 825

For this view at Luray, Link set up his camera so that when the
crossing gate was down, it acted like a giant finger pointing directly
at the retreating caboose on Train #96, creating a scene with a
powerful sense of deep space.

PLATE 78 OPPOSITE

THE BIRMINGHAM SPECIAL CROSSES BRIDGE 201, NEAR
RADFORD, VIRGINIA, DECEMBER 17, 1957, NW 1603

It was about 10:30 P.M., in mid-December 1957, and the first
section of Train #17, the *Birmingham Special*, had just stopped at
Radford before crossing this splendid steel truss bridge over the
New River. A car, on the small road beneath the bridge, has been
added for a little "human interest" in the photo.

   For years this photograph was called *The Birmingham Special
Crossing Bridge 201 East of Wurno Siding*. Link liked the name
"Wurno," which had been given to the siding because, before it
was built, there "were no" sidings there. Unfortunately, Wurno
Siding is ten miles west of Bridge 201, too far away to continue
to use that title. This is one of Link's most widely reproduced
photographs, and it was selected for the millennium edition of
Life magazine. It was also included in a *Life*-published book
documenting the achievements of the millennium, where it
represented steam railway travel.

PLATE 79 LEFT

TRAIN #2 AT SOLITUDE. NEAR ARCADIA, VIRGINIA.
FEBRUARY 9, 1957, NW 1350

Standing alone in a remote area, the sign for Solitude Siding, a section of double track for the purpose of letting trains pass, caught Link's eye as soon as he started the N&W project, but it wasn't until February 1957 that he made the photo. Link noted that "I did this shot alone, and it took a total of four hours, which was rather quick. This place was out in nowhere, and the more I studied the sign, the more alone I felt. It made me hurry to clean up and get out! It was eerie to be in total darkness in that place. It was well named—Solitude!"

PLATE 80 OPPOSITE

HIGHBALL FOR THE DOUBLEHEADER. NEAR BONSACK,
VIRGINIA, APRIL 23, 1959, NW 32K

Link's nineteenth trip to the N&W was one of his shortest (April 20–April 26, 1959), and he made the trip just to create this photograph. He was about to issue *Thunder on Blue Ridge*, the third LP of his sound recordings, and he wanted a Blue Ridge image on the cover.

By April 23, 1959, steam was rare on the N&W, and the railroad cooperated fully in helping achieve Link's vision, including the removal of the auxiliary tender between the first and second locomotives. Three cameras captured the scene, which had been planned for months and for which there was no second chance. It was raining lightly, and the photo required thirty-two #2 flashbulbs, along with three less powerful #25 bulbs to light the interior of the switchman's shack and the two lanterns, which were specially masked so as not to be too bright.

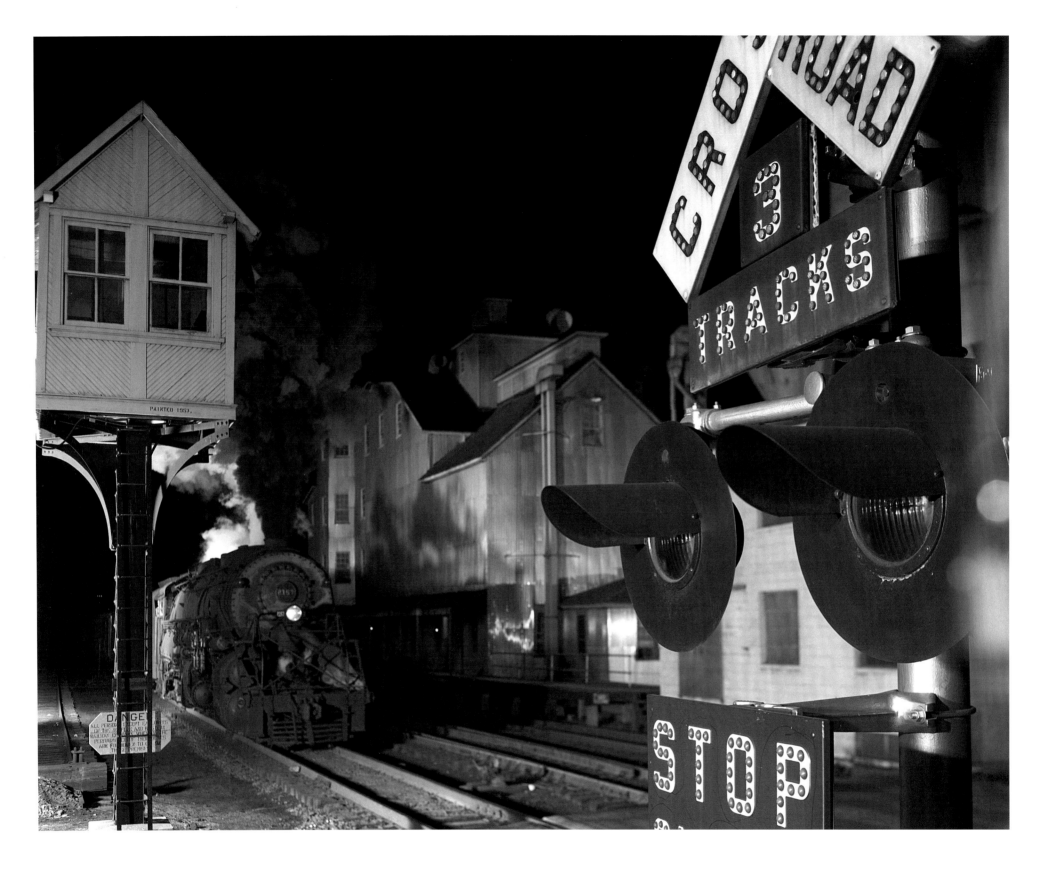

LURAY CROSSING, FIRST #51. LURAY, VIRGINIA, MARCH 23, 1956. NW 823

Few people driving on this modest street in Luray would have taken any notice of the point where the road crossed the tracks of the N&W's Shenandoah Division. What interested Link about the spot was the combination of objects he found there. These included the crossing gates and lights, the crossing watchman's shanty mounted high up on a steel column, and the strong shapes of the warehouse buildings in the background. These were all objects that had the sort of industrial geometry that Link liked to photograph. Link loved strong foreground objects pointing the way toward a scene in the background—and all of it in perfect focus. Here, a merchandise freight pulled by Class Y-6a #2157, is about to pass the camera.

JEFFERSON STREET CROSSING. ROANOKE, VIRGINIA, APRIL 16, 1955. NW 48

The Jefferson Street crossing in downtown Roanoke was located at the heart of the city and was a main thoroughfare connecting the community. Located just west of the N&W passenger station, this crossing was later eliminated.

CLASS A AND TIME FREIGHT ON A FOGGY DAY, BLUE RIDGE GRADE. NEAR BLUE RIDGE, VIRGINIA, JANUARY 1, 1959. NW 1998

On one of Link's last trips to the N&W in December 1958 and January 1959, he made tape recordings, movies, and still photos. This photo was taken the day after he made tape recordings on board Time Freight #84 and #85, between Crewe and Villamont, Virginia. Here he photographed #84 from the ground as the freight train pounds up Blue Ridge Grade. This moment is also captured in Link's movie footage.

This is what Link called a "wedge shot," in which the locomotive is large and the cars taper down to a point in the distance. He didn't care for such photos, but in this case, the gloomy day, the bulk of the engine—enlivened by a bed of steam—and the spectacular smoke and steam exhaust have turned an ordinary photo into a romantic image of steam power at its best.

BRISTOL YARD. BRISTOL, VIRGINIA, OCTOBER 20, 1956. NW 1200

Class K1 #104 with an adjacent line of freight cars fills the Bristol yard. The sun is setting and the shadows are deepening on this October day.

PLATE 85 LEFT

SWITCHER NEXT TO COLONNA'S SHIPYARD.
SOUTH NORFOLK, VIRGINIA, AUGUST 31, 1955, NW 406

At Virginia Electric Power Company's Reeve Avenue power-
generating station, Link made a series of interesting images called
Ghost Train (see NW 419A, page 21). Using timed exposures, he
captured an ethereal ghostly image of a train passing through
this industrial landscape. This daytime photo serves more
documentarian aims, recording a clear image of the transportation
industry of the day and the intersection of sea and overland freight.

PLATE 86 OPPOSITE

ABINGDON BRANCH MIXED TRAIN AT CREEK JUNCTION.
CREEK JUNCTION, VIRGINIA, OCTOBER 27, 1956,
NW 1218

The Abingdon Branch was a small line with steep grades and tight
curves. The elderly Class M was well suited to the terrain. At Creek
Junction, this doubleheader has stopped for the lead locomotive
to take water. To help with weight distribution and efficiency,
Locomotive #382 heads the train, while the second locomotive is
placed a few cars back.

PLATE 87 OVERLEAF, LEFT

TRAINS ON THE WYE AT WALTON. WALTON, VIRGINIA,
SEPTEMBER 3, 1957, NW 1402

At Walton, N&W routes from Bristol to the south and Bluefield to
the west converge. Shooting from above, Link photographed the
junction there with Class Y-6 #2138 approaching.

PLATE 88 OVERLEAF, RIGHT

FREIGHT SOUTH AT LURAY. LURAY, VIRGINIA, PROBABLY
MARCH 22, 1956, NW 850

Making an unacceptable amount of black smoke, a Class Y-5,
pulling a time freight train, speeds through Luray, headed south.
The bridge, barely visible on the left, is the same one seen from the
opposite side in *Hawksbill Creek Swimming Hole* (see plates 119
and 120). The Texaco tanks in the foreground add a non-railroad
element to this scene.

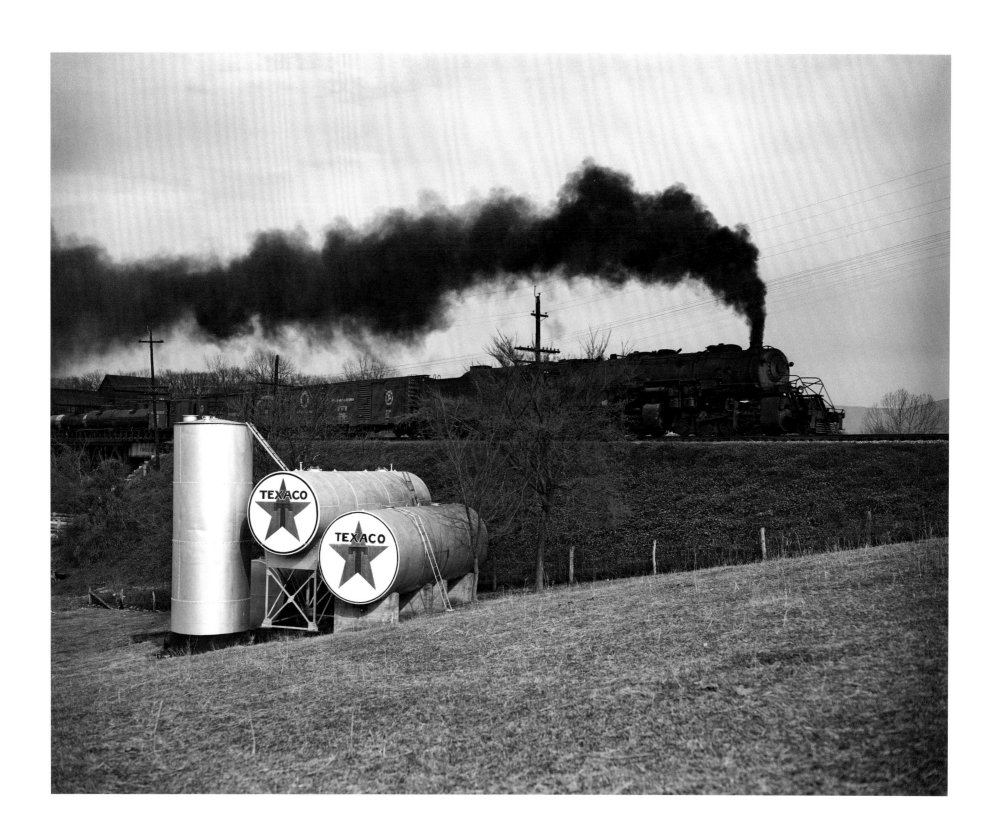

The N&W project captured the interaction between railroad and community. At the Natural Bridge station, this young boy waves enthusiastically as the caboose passes. He's greeted in return by the crew, as the freight train moves south across the river.

The Virginia Creeper, with the venerable Class M #382 on Train #202, is shown at Damascus on its afternoon run back to Abingdon, alongside what then was a modern bus of the Tennessee Coach Company. The SPECIAL destination sign on the bus suggests that it might have been on a sightseeing trip.

SECOND PIGEON CREEK SHIFTER AT
THE BORDERLAND COAL COMPANY.
MINGO COUNTY, WEST VIRGINIA,
MARCH 15, 1960, NW 2169

While at the Borderland Coal Company in West
Virginia, Y-6b #2190 shifts coal cars. Exchanging
empty hoppers for full hoppers to be delivered
to customers was the role of the Second
Pigeon Creek Shifter. Link made several audio
recordings of the engines going through the
paces of this task.

SECOND PIGEON CREEK SHIFTER AND
ICICLES. NEAR GILBERT, WEST VIRGINIA,
MARCH 16, 1960, NW 2221

This photo is dated March 16, 1960, the last
day Link made photos of steam power on the
N&W, and less than two months before all steam
locomotion was terminated on the railroad.

Steam lasted longest on the Pocahontas
and Scioto Divisions of the railroad, deep in
coal-mining country. Y-6b #2190, built in 1950,
and the most refined version of this class,
survived only another four months before being
scrapped. It is backing into the spur serving the
large Massey mine, partially seen behind the
plume of smoke and steam, to pick up a line
of coal hopper cars that have been loaded at
the mine. The coldness of the day, and maybe
of the occasion, is marked by the huge icicles.
A colorized version of this photo was used on
the cover of *2nd Pigeon and the Mocking Bird*,
volume 4 of Link's series of recordings, *Sounds
of Steam Railroading*.

W
40
35
DANGER
CLOSE CLEARANCE
DAN
ALL PERSONS E
OF THE NORFO
RAILWAY COMPA
PERFORMANCE
ARE FORBID
THIS

PLATE 93 PREVIOUS SPREAD, LEFT

PUSHER FROM REAR OF CABOOSE. BLUE RIDGE, VIRGINIA, JUNE 1958. NW 1851

A rear pusher locomotive was added behind the caboose of heavy trains ascending Blue Ridge Grade. Visible through the caboose door, Y-6b #2179 is getting the job done. Link made sound recordings of #2179 at full throttle from the caboose that day.

PLATE 94 PREVIOUS SPREAD, RIGHT

TUNNEL PORTAL AND SIGNS. WELCH, WEST VIRGINIA, AUGUST 28, 1958. NW 1883

Railroad safety is always a concern and one the N&W took seriously. Alongside a warning to stay out of this tunnel, the N&W posted the speed limit for travel through the tunnel, along the Tug River, west of Welch: forty miles per hour for passenger trains, thirty-five for freight.

PLATE 95 LEFT

CLASS A LOCOMOTIVE WITH TIME FREIGHT. VILLAMONT, VIRGINIA, 1958. NW 115C

This image appears on the cover of *Mainline to Panther*, Link's fifth and final album of N&W railroad sounds. One side of the LP is devoted to recordings made on Train #84, eastbound, and Train #85, westbound, the freight service between Crewe and Roanoke, Virginia.

PLATE 96 OPPOSITE

EMD GP-9 WITH PASSENGER TRAIN #25. VILLAMONT, VIRGINIA, 1958. NW 114C

As the era of steam ended, many parts of the landscape were becoming obsolete. No longer were water towers needed or used to fill the tender with water to make steam to power the locomotive. An EMD GP-9 passes through Villamont, with Train #25.

OPPOSITE

LEAVING THE MAIN LINE FOR THE
ABINGDON BRANCH. ABINGDON,
VIRGINIA, OCTOBER 21, 1956, NW 1201

The Abingdon Branch trains passed this
water tank just moments before leaving
the Bristol line to enter the northern end of
the Abingdon Branch in Abingdon, Virginia.
Link took this photograph in October 1956,
but apparently never printed it. The image
was discovered among his negatives by
Thomas H. Garver, Link's agent at the time,
and printed by Mary L. Bachmann, Link's
assistant and printer, for an exhibition, which
opened in December 2000. Link died the
following month. Only two signed copies of
this photograph exist.

PLATE 98 RIGHT

ABINGDON BRANCH MIXED TRAIN
CROSSING BRIDGE 8. WATAUGA,
VIRGINIA, NOVEMBER 1, 1957, NW 1522

According to Link's notes, this image
captures Class M #382 crossing Bridge 8
along the Abingdon Branch. The route of the
Abingdon Branch followed the path of local
creeks and rivers to provide the gentlest
grades through this remote area. Numerous
bridges crossed both water and land.

PLATE 99 LEFT
COAL HOPPERS AND SIGN. NEAR CHRISTIANSBURG, VIRGINIA, 1956,
NW 121K

Montgomery Tunnel was a favorite location on Christiansburg Grade for Link. He photographed here both at night and during the day and made a number of tape recordings as well. There was a heavy grade in the westward direction, so trains exiting from the west portal of the tunnel were working hard. This photo is unusual in that Link has turned his camera away from the tunnel to catch the splendid exhaust of a westbound train of empty coal hoppers in the afternoon sunlight. The round sign in silhouette is a speed limit warning sign to eastbound trains coming downgrade and about to enter the tunnel.

PLATE 100 OPPOSITE
THE POWHATAN ARROW WESTBOUND ON BRIDGE 854.
COOPER, WEST VIRGINIA, JULY 27, 1955, NW 5K

On a warm summer afternoon in 1955, Class J #604 smartly pulled the *Powhatan Arrow*, the N&W's best train, across Bridge 854, above the Bluestone River, west of Cooper Tunnel. The faded red of the old heavyweight mail storage car behind the tender contrasts with the line of modern Tuscan red coaches and a lounge-diner, moving swiftly from Norfolk to Cincinnati. Neither mail nor checked baggage was normally carried on this train, as the N&W didn't want to disturb the hard-driving fifteen-and-a-half-hour schedule between the two cities.

PLATE 101 OVERLEAF, LEFT
GREEN COVE STATION FROM THE FIREMAN'S POSITION.
GREEN COVE, VIRGINIA, JUNE 17, 1955, NW 177

Each crew member has a unique vantage point of the passing community. Link wanted to capture the subtle differences in angle and position. Here he recorded the fireman's position as the Class M approached the Green Cove station.

PLATE 102 OVERLEAF, RIGHT
ABINGDON BRANCH MIXED TRAIN ON BRIDGE 52. WHITE TOP,
VIRGINIA, OCTOBER 27, 1956, NW 1228

The Abingdon Branch ran for approximately fifty-five miles between Abingdon, Virginia, and West Jefferson, North Carolina. In that stretch, bridges were common, spanning valleys, springs, creeks, and rivers. Taken from water level, this image looks up at Bridge 52 as Train #201, with two locomotives, passes by, headed to White Top, the highest point on the Abingdon line.

WHITE TOP STATION. WHITE TOP, VIRGINIA,
OCTOBER 1956, NW 1278

Class M #382 has brought Train #201
southbound into the White Top station. This
was not only the highest point on the Abingdon
Branch, but also, at 3,565 feet above sea level,
the highest point reached by any regularly
scheduled passenger train east of the
Rocky Mountains.

Today, this is the southern terminus of the
Virginia Creeper Trail for hikers and bicyclists,
and the original station, demolished in the
1970s, has been reconstructed. The Creeper
Trail is popular with bicyclists who want either
a tough or an easy ride. It's tough peddling
upgrade from Damascus, Virginia, to White Top,
but a nice, easy glide downgrade.

LOOKING DOWN ON LOCOMOTIVE #382.
NELLA, NORTH CAROLINA, NOVEMBER 1,
1957, NW 1511

Perched on an overlook along the Abingdon
Branch, Link peered down on Class M #382
as it passed. Steep grades and tight curves
resulted from the light-duty construction of the
Abingdon Branch. The scenery was some of the
most striking to Link's eye, with bridges, roaring
creeks, and narrow valleys. While the railroad
used the name Nella, the town was also called
Husk, which was the postal service's name for it.

PLATE 105 LEFT

APPROACHING GREEN COVE. GREEN COVE, VIRGINIA,
JUNE 17, 1955, NW 135

Green Cove is a small town located along the Abingdon Branch
that was served predominantly by the N&W. In this image, shot
with Link's Rolleiflex handheld camera, the train approaches Green
Cove, with a whistle sign in the foreground.

PLATE 106 OPPOSITE

EASTBOUND FREIGHT PASSING ON THE MAIN LINE.
ABINGDON, VIRGINIA, JUNE 18, 1955, NW 292

The Abingdon Branch left the Bristol line of the N&W just east of
the Abingdon station. On its return to Abingdon, the train entered
the Bristol line, passing the siding (an area of double tracks for
the purpose of letting a faster train pass), and proceeded a short
distance west to the passenger station. After a brief stop there,
it moved to the west end of the siding. After riding it all day, Link
had access to the whole of the train, and he made this photograph
from the cab roof of Class M #429, while the train waited for Time
Freight #88 to pass.

Link's presence atop the cab was apparently noticed by the
engineer of the Class Y-6a #2161 at the head end of the freight
train, who told his fireman to have a look, for both men are waving
to the Abingdon Branch engine crew.

in undertaking his Norfolk and Western project, O. Winston Link sought to document the last major steam-powered railroad in America before the coming of the diesel. He succeeded in his aim, creating what may be the greatest view of the late age of steam on the American railroad. He garnered a photographic, sound, and film portfolio that, as has already been mentioned, Tom Garver called "his own advertising campaign for the steam locomotive." He also focused on his father's homeland, the parts of the N&W system running through the Appalachian Mountains and their foothills.

But Link captured more than the age of steam on the N&W. His photos depict life along that railroad, often with area residents prominently featured in or around their houses, farms, and places of business. The images also show local folks at play, in places such as drive-in movie theaters and public swimming pools. The people in his images, through project-wide choices that were intentional on Link's part, work against the dirt-poor image of Appalachia depicted by the FSA/OWI photographers during the Great Depression and the early years of World War II; in movies of the time, such as Arthur Ripley's *Thunder Road* from 1958; and later through "War on Poverty" government programs, announced by President Lyndon B. Johnson in 1964, and in writings by authors such as Breece D'J Pancake and Lee Smith. As mentioned earlier, Link associate Ben Halpern observed, "Notice that everyone looks comfortable and middle-class. You don't see any tension or unhappiness, even among the teenagers."

Link knew that the steam locomotives he was documenting would vanish, and his depiction of Appalachian small-town life as idyllic was intentional. What he apparently did not realize was that he was documenting another aspect of American culture just

before a major transition: the virtual end of commercial activity in many small American towns, with all of the economic and social implications that followed. It does not seem that Link and his assistants realized how utterly Appalachian—indeed, American—small-town life would change during the four decades following the end of his Norfolk and Western project. Ironically, by following a theme of change, that of the transition from steam to diesel on the American railroad, Link also captured a small-town milieu that was itself on the verge of dramatic transformation.

As Garver stated in 1996, "I knew that the engines we were documenting would never return, but I was not aware then that forty years would so completely transform the towns and their people. Somehow in my mind they had become a fixed quantity." [82]

Communities such as Abingdon, which had the advantage of tourism or perhaps a local college or university, managed to make their way in a new era of better road transportation, deindustrialization, mechanization of extractive resource industries such as coal mining, and the exhaustion or economic obsolescence of extractive resources such as coal and timber. But many small towns in North Carolina, Virginia, and West Virginia, and throughout the United States, did not fare as well as Abingdon.

These changes transformed many of the communities depicted in Link's photos. Green Cove and White Top, Virginia, for example, became essentially ghost towns in the 1970s and '80s; however, they are now popular tourist stop-offs along the Virginia Creeper Trail.[83] The drive-in at Iaeger, West Virginia, like most American drive-ins, closed long ago. The station at Rural Retreat, Virginia, sits empty and forlorn. Lansing and West Jefferson, North Carolina, survive as local centers of commerce but Nella (Husk), North Carolina, too far from the Virginia Creeper Trail and the New River to be of interest to tourists, is virtually deserted today.

There are no Amtrak passenger trains on any of the N&W lines Link depicted, so the fine passenger service and the friendly local stations available to railroad patrons in Link's photos have vanished. In most of this region today, the automobile is the only convenient transportation option.

Fortunately, we have Link's photos. They not only show us what was—a time of small farms, local stores, and a transportation alternative for those who could not, or did not wish to, drive—but also what, if we have the will as a society, may be possible.

Plates 107 to 152 demonstrate Link stepping back from a focus on the trains, even farther than Hastings and his colleagues, to show life in the Appalachian portion of the N&W's service area. Despite emphasis on Appalachian life, Link used the steam-powered trains of the N&W as a recurring, unifying theme—there is one, more or less obvious, in almost all of these wonderful photographs.

Plates 107 to 126 are carefully composed night images (along with two daytime photos of important night scenes)—the type of photograph that made Link famous. Among them are a number of excellent views—such as *The Log Cabin* (plate 107) and *Train Moving by the Whitehouse Church* (plate 112)—that are little known, and a number of interesting variants of well-known Link images. Some of these, in this observer's view, are better than the well-known ones—compare plate 110 with the famous *Hester Fringer's Living Room on the Tracks* (NW 720; see page 28): The sour-faced mother is gone, and the image simply shows a boy surrounded by his pets and entranced by a passing train. Another example is

plate 122. Compare it with the familiar *Egg Stove and Bananas Vesuvius, Virginia* (NW 1352; see page 148), in which the woman behind the counter has her eyes closed. Perhaps the most fasci nating variant here is plate 116—the blank screen shows that the celebrated *Hotshot Eastbound* (NW 1103; see page 22) is actually a photomontage; Link had to tip in an image onto the screen, which was washed out by the light of his flashbulbs, and later printed the photo from a copy negative of the photomontage print. Plates 11 and 119 are followed by daytime Link photographs of both loca tions, forming an interesting comparison. This sequence of nigh shots closes with a photo of a tabby cat, an N&W pet, enjoying a meal on a railroad office desk.

Plates 128 to 135 are images of life along the N&W during daylight hours. Plate 128, taken in the Roanoke, Virginia, station that now houses the O. Winston Link Museum, shows the sta tion before another transition that was imminent in the 1950s—an African American man sits in the "colored" waiting room, reading a newspaper. In these images, people wait for passenger trains serving an area that is now bereft of rail passenger service, or watch trains from stations that have long since vanished or have been con verted to nonrailroad uses. This sequence closes with plate 135 showing a boy standing in front of a grocery store with a picture window adorned with faded letters spelling out Link's initials: O W L Reflected in the window is the silhouette of a steam engine.

As in the previous chapter, the last sequence is a look a Link's beloved Abingdon Branch and the Virginia Creeper (plates 136 to 151). Many of the images show passengers served by the branch's mixed train. A recurrent theme in the images is a man picking up the mail directly from the Creeper as it wends its way

EGG STOVE AND BANANAS. VESUVIUS. VIRGINIA. FEBRUARY 10. 1957. NW 1352

to and from West Jefferson, North Carolina (see plates 139, 140, 141, and 148).

Plates 142 to 145 are a constructed sequence depicting the tiny, isolated village of Nella (Husk), North Carolina. A cow walks down the main street by the store; a woman, possibly the storekeeper, looks out as Jimbo, "the hound of Husk," watches the photographer from the stairs of the general store; a train thunders by; and a "Stairway to Nowhere" presages the future of this community.[84]

The Virginia Creeper sequence closes with a Currier and Ives–like pastoral of the little train passing a farm field still resplendent with shocks of corn, while workers load shucked corn into a horse-drawn wagon—amazingly for the 1950s (plate 151). The chapter closes with a non-railroad image that is not of comfortable and middle-class subjects, but they are smiling: Two miners, one with a coal-dust-besmirched face and the other with a crooked tooth, pose for Link's camera.

PLATE 107 OPPOSITE

THE LOG CABIN. MIDVALE, VIRGINIA, JULY 30, 1955, NW 359

By posing a man in front of this vacant cabin, Link created a picturesque rural scene that combined the railroad and the life around it. Train #96, pulled by Class Y-6 #2134, passes Midvale, northbound.

PLATE 108 RIGHT

FATHER AND SON AT MONTGOMERY TUNNEL. NEAR CHRISTIANSBURG, VIRGINIA, DECEMBER 14, 1955, NW 704

Link asked C. E. "Jack" Hash of the N&W's advertising department if he and his young son, Dan, would like to be in one of his photographs. Hash accepted, and this image of father and son has become one of Link's most popular. By having two figures in the scene, Link has both established the space and given the scene a human touch. Two generations stand awestruck by the thunderous power of Class Y-5 #2110 roaring out of the tunnel and pounding upgrade, westbound.

The site is the west portal of Montgomery Tunnel, which is actually twin tunnels, 663 feet long, with each track of the double-tracked main line in its own separate bore.

PLATE 109 OVERLEAF, LEFT

TRAIN #2 NORTH AT FRINGER'S MILL. LITHIA, VIRGINIA, DECEMBER 15, 1955, NW 712

Link asked Bobby Goggin, a lad from Lithia, to be included in this image made at Fringer's Mill. The derelict mill, with its rusty iron waterwheel, appealed to Link's fascination with old machinery, and Goggin adds the usual note of human vitality. In the background, Train #2 is heading north.

PLATE 110 OVERLEAF, RIGHT

HESTER FRINGER'S LIVING ROOM. LITHIA, VIRGINIA, DECEMBER 16, 1955, NW 716

When Hester Fringer moved into this old house in Lithia, just a few feet from the tracks of the N&W's Shenandoah Division, she immediately had a larger window put into the living room so that she would have a better view of the passing trains. This is a variation of the better-known photo (see page 28), and features the family pets as Fringer's grandson, George Poulis, gives a good wave to a passing train. The pets took little notice of the rumble of the frequently passing trains.

PLATE 111 OPPOSITE

TRAIN #77 WESTBOUND. SHAWSVILLE,
VIRGINIA, DECEMBER 18, 1955,
NW 722

A rush of speed punctuates the ancient,
slow-moving ritual of bringing in the cows.
All but obscured by clouds of steam, smoke,
and dust, a Class A leads Train #77 west.
This is a scene that required remarkable
insight to visualize, as it looked so different
during the day.

PLATE 112 RIGHT

TRAIN MOVING BY THE WHITEHOUSE
CHURCH. SHAWSVILLE, VIRGINIA,
DECEMBER 20, 1955, NW 731

Train #3, the *Pocahontas*, rushes westbound
in the background, as Nancy the pony pulls
a wagon carrying Denny and Harry Hayes
and Sonny Westmoreland, while Spike the
dog runs alongside, past the Whitehouse
Church in Shawsville, on a cold December
night. The church is no longer standing.

PLATE 113 LEFT

FREIGHT TRAIN #88 NORTH AT GOOSENECK DAM.
BUENA VISTA, VIRGINIA, MARCH 30, 1956, NW 884

Gooseneck Dam, an abandoned electric power dam later swept away by a flood, was a few miles north of Buffalo Forge, Virginia, on the N&W's Shenandoah Division. This photo, unquestionably the most complicated and difficult of all of Link's photos made on the N&W, could have been created only in the spring of the year, when the river was up and before the trees along the right of way on the opposite bank had leafed out. Here is Link's description of this photo:

> It required six full days to set up and complete. To get the flash units across the river we had to cross on a two-wire span, one for your feet and the higher one for your hands, as there were no boats or bridges nearby. The uptilted strata with water rushing between the plates of rock in the set-up area was so confusing at night that we set up guide ropes to get to the light stands and cameras. It was a great challenge, and a satisfaction to see the negative of the first exposure, without any test, was as we had calculated it to be.

PLATE 114 OPPOSITE

SECOND 95 MOVING SOUTH WITH CHILDREN. LITHIA,
VIRGINIA, JULY 30, 1956, NW 1083

Mr. Mungo Buchanan owned a home that faced the N&W's Shenandoah Division. The grounds had a quaint little "Japanese bridge," which crossed Back Creek. Here, the three children of Mrs. Helen Keith try their hand at fishing in the creek as Class Y-6a #2157 pulls Second 95, southbound.

DARLENE KEITH AT THE WATER PUMP AT MUNGO
BUCHANAN'S HOUSE. LITHIA, VIRGINIA, AUGUST 1, 1956,
NW 1088

Mungo Buchanan owned a home with substantial gardens adjacent to the N&W's Shenandoah Division main line in Lithia. Link worked here in late July and early August 1956, making several photos of Darlene Keith and other area children at play, while N&W trains passed in the background.

The water in Lithia was highly charged with minerals and regarded as a health tonic. Here on the porch, Darlene pumps water into a jug as an N&W freight passes in the background.

HOTSHOT EASTBOUND. IAEGER, WEST VIRGINIA,
AUGUST 2, 1956, NW 1104

On the hot night of August 2, 1956, Link created what has become his most famous photograph. The Iaeger Drive-In was located on the N&W's main line, and the movie that evening was *Battle Taxi*, a film about the Korean War. Link placed Willie Allen and Dorothy Christian in his 1952 Buick convertible, and set the view camera above the car on an extension tripod. The camera was then adjusted to place the image in perfect focus from about six feet away to infinity. This image is a variant of the more famous NW 1103 (see page 22), which depicts a plane on the movie screen.

SOMETIMES THE ELECTRICITY FAILS.
VESUVIUS, VIRGINIA, AUGUST 6, 1956,
NW 1124

Mr. and Mrs. Edgar Austin operated the
general store in an old building in Vesuvius
that faced the tracks of the N&W's
Shenandoah Division. Link quickly spotted
the gravity gas pump (now on display at the
O. Winston Link Museum), and was delighted
to find that it was still operational, even
though a modern electric gas pump stood
just a few feet away. He was told that it was
kept on standby because "sometimes the
electricity fails."

In early August 1956, Bob Cullen and
Jane Groah, sweethearts who later married,
sit in Link's Buick convertible as W. A.
Miller fills the glass gravity reservoir with a
hand pump. In the background, seemingly
unnoticed by everyone, a freight train passes.

TIME FREIGHT PASSES VESUVIUS
STATION. VESUVIUS, VIRGINIA,
AUGUST 1956. NW 1136

Class Y-6a #2164 passes the Vesuvius
general store, seen on the left. Link made a
number of images in and around this store,
including several variants of the gravity-fed
gas pump outside. In this image Link's trailer
and an array of lighting equipment are visible.

PLATE 119 LEFT
HAWKSBILL CREEK SWIMMING HOLE.
LURAY, VIRGINIA, AUGUST 9, 1956,
NW 1128

This is a variation of the better-known
version of *Hawksbill Creek Swimming Hole*,
which shows a large freight locomotive
on the high bridge. Here Class K-2a #129
is pulling the N&W's Train #2 northbound
to Hagerstown and then on, via the
Pennsylvania Railroad, to New York City.
Link asked Barry Good and the Judd
children to stay up late on this evening in
August 1956, as Train #2 was not scheduled
to pass through Luray until 11:41 P.M.

PLATE 120 OPPOSITE
HAWKSBILL CREEK SWIMMING HOLE
BY DAY. LURAY, VIRGINIA,
MARCH 22, 1956, NW 114K

This photo, made at Hawksbill Creek in
Luray, illustrates the problems Link faced
when working in daylight. Despite the
powerful elements of the two bridges and
train, the details of the locomotive are all
but lost in the photograph because the
sun was at the wrong angle. Furthermore,
the rocky streambed is overlighted and
appears lifeless and unappealing. This is a
dreary industrial landscape compared with
Hawksbill Creek Swimming Hole, made
at night a few months later (plate 119). At
night, Link was able to completely reshape
this landscape into an appealing scene.

PLATE 121 LEFT

MAIN STREET AND TRAIN #2 NORTH, STANLEY, VIRGINIA, JANUARY 31, 1957, NW 1343

This image is the result of Link's vision combined with good communication and cooperation all around. Link recognized that, with dramatic lighting, he could change the appearance of the main street of an ordinary little town into a setting of high visual drama. The people in Stanley cooperated fully in helping with the setup, including letting Link and his crew take refuge under the marquee of the local movie theater. Link telephoned the N&W dispatcher in Roanoke from the phone booth seen in the photo, to check on the progress of oncoming trains. The N&W cooperated by holding up two freight trains, which were due to follow each other in rapid succession, so that the photographer would have time to change the numerous flashbulbs spread across the scene, including one in the phone booth.

PLATE 122 OPPOSITE

EGG STOVE AND BANANAS, VESUVIUS, VIRGINIA, FEBRUARY 10, 1957, NW 1355

The general store in Vesuvius was run by Mr. and Mrs. Edgar Austin, seen behind the counter. The "egg" in the title of the photo is a play on words that Link enjoyed. It refers not to something that the store might sell, such as bananas, but to the shape of the Burnside No. 1 stove, cast by the Bristol Foundry Company in Bristol, Virginia, and known in the area as a "Bristol egg." The counter, scale, and stove were saved and now reside in the O. Winston Link Museum in Roanoke, Virginia.

In the foreground, W. A. Miller, seen pumping gas in Link's photo *Sometimes the Electricity Fails* (plate 117), is talking to eighty-four-year-old Thurston A. Graves, who served fifty-seven years on the N&W, starting in 1888. Class K-2a #127 is visible through the window. Walter Finney, who was engineer that evening, stopped the train exactly where Link wanted it.

PLATE 123 OPPOSITE

GIANT OAK. MAX MEADOWS. VIRGINIA. DECEMBER 30. 1957.
NW 1643

This photograph was made on December 30, 1957, the next-to-last night for steam-powered passenger trains on the N&W's line to Bristol, Virginia. The *Birmingham Special* didn't stop at Max Meadows, but would have passed by here about 11 P.M. Link set up enough lights to illuminate the train, but he may have been most fascinated with the huge oak in the foreground, which stood alone in a meadow. Here's what he wrote about this photo:

> We were hoping to get an owl in the tree, but lighting 360 feet of rail made problems enough. The circumference of the tree was 18 feet, 6 inches, making the diameter very close to six feet!

PLATE 124 RIGHT

TRAIN #42 PASSING THE RESIDENCE OF MR. AND MRS.
B. F. POPE. MAX MEADOWS, VIRGINIA. DECEMBER 31. 1957,
NW 1645

The Popes lived in a substantial Victorian home just west of Max Meadows. Link had spotted the porch (later demolished), with its fancy turned spindles and good view of the tracks, and recognized it as a perfect foreground for a photo. On December 31, 1957, Mr. and Mrs. Pope and their dog stood close together on the porch to watch the final passage of steam-powered passenger trains in front of their home. This was Train #42, the *Pelican*, which would have passed by about 10:30 P.M., moving eastward toward Roanoke. The next day, January 1, 1958, diesels took over all passenger runs on the line between Bristol and Roanoke.

PLATE 125 LEFT

WELCH SWIMMING POOL. WELCH, WEST VIRGINIA.
AUGUST 28, 1958. NW 1961

By August 1958, Link's work was well known to all of the employees of the N&W. Link had told the dispatcher on the Pocahontas Division where he would be working on the evening of August 28, and the engine crews had been instructed to make sure they weren't making much smoke as they passed the municipal swimming pool in Welch, the county seat of McDowell County, West Virginia.

This is the second swimming pool photo Link attempted, and the lighting and composition are much surer than in the previous one, made near Bluefield, West Virginia, two summers previously. Here, four young local women chat with the big-city boy from New York, Leroy "Corky" Zider, Link's teenage nephew and one of his best assistants.

PLATE 126 OPPOSITE

MAIN LINE ON MAIN STREET. NORTH FORK, WEST VIRGINIA,
AUGUST 29, 1958. NW 1964

The heyday of many of the coal towns in West Virginia's Mercer, McDowell, and Mingo Counties was during the first two decades of the twentieth century. As a result, many of the small coal towns had very substantial buildings, but the valleys were so narrow that the railroad, roadways, and buildings competed for the same space. By the 1950s, work in the mines had diminished, and the population was dropping. Most of the buildings in this photograph were empty by then, and all have since been demolished.

Here, a heavy freight, pulled by Class Y-6b #2189, thunders east on the main line at full throttle. In this variant of the more famous NW 1966, Link has placed three kids on the front steps of the abandoned bank, and the doctor's office on the third floor next door is dark.

PLATE 127 PREVIOUS SPREAD, LEFT

CAT ALONE ON TABLE. NATURAL BRIDGE STATION, VIRGINIA, MARCH 1, 1956, NW 972

Always attuned to the animals he encountered, Link made sure to photograph this N&W cat, dining on the food left by the crew. Seemingly well fed and not the least skittish, this cat seems to know that it belongs.

PLATE 128 PREVIOUS SPREAD, RIGHT

MAN IN ROANOKE STATION WAITING ROOM. ROANOKE, VIRGINIA, JUNE 19, 1955, NW 308

The N&W passenger station was modernized by famed industrial designer Raymond Loewy between 1947 and 1949. For the duration of Link's project, segregation was still common in the South, including the passenger waiting area. Sitting in the "colored" waiting room, an unidentified man waits beneath the large glass clock.

PLATE 129 OPPOSITE

INTERIOR OF ROANOKE STATION. ROANOKE, VIRGINIA, AUGUST 1956, NW 1170

Passengers await the arrival of a train in this view of the west end of the concourse at N&W's Roanoke passenger station, now the site of the O. Winston Link Museum. The concourse, which extended over the station's four tracks, was later removed. However, the windows seen in the distance were preserved and then reinstalled at their present location on the O. Winston Link Museum's south wall, providing a view of the current Norfolk Southern train operations.

PLATE 130 RIGHT

T. H. HANKINS HOLDING UP HIS SON ON THE FENCE AS A SWITCHER PASSES. ROANOKE, VIRGINIA, APRIL 17, 1955, NW 37

Railroads, in general, and steam locomotives, in particular, have long attracted people of all generations. Here, T. H. Hankins holds his son up on the fence at the busy Jefferson Street Crossing, to watch a yard engine as it darts about during its switching duties at the Roanoke passenger station. The Hotel Roanoke is visible in the background.

PLATE 131 PREVIOUS SPREAD, LEFT

WYTHEVILLE STATION WITH APPROACHING TRAIN.
WYTHEVILLE, VIRGINIA, 1957, NW 1696

Customers await the arrival of an eastbound passenger train,
probably #46, the *Tennessean*, at the modernized Wytheville
station, on the Bristol line. During the late 1940s, this station, along
with several others, underwent a major renovation as part of post–
World War II improvements.

PLATE 132 PREVIOUS SPREAD, RIGHT

THREE YOUNG BOYS WATCHING A TRAIN. NATURAL BRIDGE
STATION, VIRGINIA, MARCH 1, 1956, NW 964

At the Natural Bridge station, three young boys watch a mixed
freight train, with coal hoppers, rolling south over the James River.

PLATE 133 OPPOSITE

LOG CABIN. MIDVALE, VIRGINIA, DECEMBER 11, 1955,
NW 686

Link spotted this ancient log cabin along the N&W's Shenandoah
Division and returned to photograph it while a train passed to
complete the scene. During the course of this trip to the N&W,
he made several photographs of the Harless cabin. A similar one
includes James Harless, the cabin owner, gathering firewood.

PLATE 134 RIGHT

EASTBOUND LOADED COAL TRAIN. CAMBRIA, VIRGINIA,
SEPTEMBER 3, 1957, NW 1393

Pedestrians wait as a Class Y-6 passes through a crossing at
Cambria, near the summit of the Christiansburg Grade. Link was
impressed with this N&W station and described it as "handsome"
on the envelope containing the original negative.

PLATE 135 LEFT
KID WATCHING IN FRONT OF OWENS
GROCERY STORE. BLUEFIELD.
WEST VIRGINIA, OCTOBER 6, 1955,
NW 470

Continuing the series of photographs of
moving Class G-1 #7 to a park for permanent
exhibition (see plates 27 and 32), Link turned
his camera to the audience that the event
had attracted. This young onlooker follows
the movement of the engine as its reflection
appears in the window of Owens Grocery on
Bluefield Avenue.

PLATE 136 OPPOSITE
MRS. WILCOX HOLDING HER SON.
LANSING, NORTH CAROLINA,
JUNE 18, 1955, NW 252

Betty Wilcox looks at the passing scenery of
the Abingdon Branch, while her son, Curtis,
sleeps on her lap. Curtis slept peacefully
throughout the short series of images Link
made during this trip.

PLATE 137 PREVIOUS SPREAD, LEFT

KIDS EATING, DRINKING, AND TALKING ON TRAIN. WEST JEFFERSON, NORTH CAROLINA, OCTOBER 1957, NW 1481

Link made a number of photographs of the kids enjoying their field trip from Bristol Junior High School. Unusual for Train #201, this trip contained a passenger car, a baggage car, and a combine car. The combine car was likely added for the students.

PLATE 138 PREVIOUS SPREAD, RIGHT

LAUNDRY ON THE LINE NEAR DAMASCUS STATION. DAMASCUS, VIRGINIA, JUNE 17, 1955, NW 119

The N&W's Abingdon Branch was not only rugged railroading but also an intimate part of the domestic and urban life of the towns and people it served for decades. Out of respect for the freshly washed laundry hung daringly close to the tracks, the locomotive slips by while making as little smoke as possible.

PLATE 139 LEFT

PICKING UP THE MAIL FOR KONNAROCK. CREEK JUNCTION, VIRGINIA, JUNE 18, 1955, NW 230

Creek Junction won't be found on any road maps. It was a stop on the Abingdon Branch where a spur track once ran to the lumber town of Konnarock, Virginia. This line had long since been pulled up, but the train still stopped at Creek Junction to take on water and to drop off and pick up the mail for Konnarock.

PLATE 140 OPPOSITE

PICKING UP THE MAIL AT GREEN COVE. GREEN COVE, VIRGINIA, OCTOBER 27, 1956, NW 1231

This photo was taken just seconds after the much more famous image *Old Maude Bows to the Virginia Creeper*, as Train #201 arrived in Green Cove (see page 9). The train is now stopped, and Maude has raised her head as a man walks by to pick up the mail for Green Cove and the surrounding area.

CHARLIE DOLLINGER CARRIES MAIL. WHITE TOP, VIRGINIA,
JUNE 17, 1955, NW 271

When this photograph was made in June 1955, Charlie Dollinger
was White Top's postman. For thirty-two years he had been picking
up the mail from the morning train, Abingdon Branch Train #201,
and delivering the town's mail to the afternoon train, #202. Here,
with mailbag in hand, he waits for the northbound Creeper. It
was due at White Top at 1:06 P.M., but was sometimes hours late,
depending on the amount of freight being handled on the line. The
freight had precedence over maintaining a regular schedule and the
convenience of passengers in this relaxed backcountry area.

COW WALKING DOWN MAIN STREET. NELLA,
NORTH CAROLINA, OCTOBER 1957, NW 1503

Always a fan of animals, Link made sure to photograph this cow
walking down the street along the tracks in the town of Nella (Husk).

WOMAN AND JIMBO AT THE STORE. NELLA,
NORTH CAROLINA, OCTOBER 1957, NW 1515A

Link loved the Abingdon Branch for its scenery, but he also loved
Jimbo, nicknamed "the hound of Husk," because of his propensity
for howling every time an Abingdon Branch train arrived. Watched
by Jimbo and the storekeeper inside, Link made several images of
this tiny town along the tracks.

TRAIN #202 APPROACHES NELLA. NELLA,
NORTH CAROLINA, OCTOBER 1, 1957, NW 1550

With the steep grades of the Abingdon Branch, a doubleheader
was sometimes required. Train #202 passes through Nella (Husk),
northbound toward Abingdon.

PLATE 145 LEFT

STAIRWAY TO NOWHERE. NELLA, NORTH CAROLINA,
OCTOBER 1, 1957, NW 1547

Dilapidated and derelict, this useless stairway in the town of Nella
(Husk) was discovered by Link in 1957. With no destination, there
seems to be no real purpose for the stairs. This remnant of bygone
days captured Link's imagination.

PLATE 146 OPPOSITE

RUNNING BETWEEN NELLA AND TUCKERDALE.
NORTH CAROLINA, OCTOBER 22, 1956, NW 1249

In a scene that might be described as a perfect image of "domestic
rusticity," double-headed Abingdon Branch Train #201 moves
through the hills south of Nella (Husk). The route took the train past
many small farms and rural homes on its way to Tuckerdale, and
then on to West Jefferson, North Carolina.

PLATE 147 OVERLEAF, LEFT

YOUNG BOY PUMPING WATER AS TRAIN PASSES.
TUCKERDALE, NORTH CAROLINA, OCTOBER 17, 1955,
NW 648

On the Abingdon Branch at Tuckerdale, a young boy pumps water
from a well, as the Virginia Creeper passes in the background.
This intimate view of the boy's chore reflects the proximity of the
railroad to the people dependent on it.

PLATE 148 OVERLEAF, RIGHT

WAITING ON MAIL AT THE LANSING STATION. LANSING,
NORTH CAROLINA, OCTOBER 22, 1956, NW 1254

The mountain town of Lansing consisted of one row of business
buildings facing the classic board-and-batten N&W station, which
was located just a few feet from Big Horse Creek. Here, Train #202,
northbound, is just pulling into the station. The locomotive will pull
forward far enough to position the passenger car and baggage-
mail car right by the station.

BROWN'S BOTTOM. DAMASCUS. VIRGINIA.
OCTOBER 29. 1956. NW 1266

Farmers Dave Stout and Roy Phipps load dried
corn onto their ancient wagon as Abingdon
Branch Train #202, northbound, passes in the
late afternoon sunlight. Link, a man from the
city, was fascinated to find that farming was
still practiced here as he had seen it in the
lithographs created by Currier and Ives in the
mid-nineteenth century. Link had found a vision
of an old America, and was pleased to know
that he was preserving it for history.

Train #202, pulled by Class M #382, had an
unusually large load on this October day, which
indicates that this photo was made in a valley
called Brown's Bottom, between Damascus
and Abingdon, Virginia. South of Damascus,
the grades were much steeper, and beyond
that point, Abingdon Branch locomotives were
usually limited to no more than five freight cars,
plus the passenger and baggage-mail cars.
There are five empty hopper cars in the train,
indicating that coal had been brought in for the
approaching winter.

MINERS JAMES BAILEY AND RAY
BUTCHER. GILBERT. WEST VIRGINIA.
MARCH 18. 1960. NW 2215

The N&W was not just about trains and the
people who operated them. The N&W was
about coal. Coal both powered its locomotives
and provided its greatest source of revenue.
Mines served by the N&W provided coal used
for heating, power generation, and steelmaking,
domestically and abroad.

Throughout the course of O. Winston Link's Norfolk and Western project, his technical and artistic methods stood in contrast to the common practices of the times. As Link worked on the project, his equipment was becoming less common. Like most prominent railroad-subject photographers before him—Lucius Beebe is the prime example—Link primarily used a view camera. The camera made wonderful photos but was difficult to operate, required deliberate setup activity, and took relatively expensive film that was hard to load. For quick work, Link used a Rolleiflex roll-film camera. He would undoubtedly have considered its medium-format negatives to be small.

But the advent of the 35mm camera was changing the way photography was done in the 1940s and '50s. High-quality 35mm cameras made images that, while in some ways technically limited compared to those produced by large-format cameras, could be of superb quality in the hands of a skilled photographer. Before the advent of the 35mm, small cameras, such as the various Kodak Brownie models, were fixed-lens units intended for amateur photographers taking "snapshots." The 35mm also required less experience to operate than view cameras, and many models were lower in cost than the types of cameras Link used.

So railroad-subject photographers who followed Link, and many professional photographers in the generation after his, used the 35mm camera as their primary photographic platform. Link didn't really transition to the 35mm camera—although some photos in the N&W series are 35mm negatives, none of the artistically significant ones are in that format.

Link's style, as has already been mentioned, was also becoming anachronistic in the 1950s. He followed the grand posed advertising photography tradition, while most art photographers—Link did not see himself as such, perhaps, but today we compare him to his art photographer contemporaries—in the generation after his, gravitated to the street photography movement (also known as candid photography or real life reportage) popularized by Robert Frank and Henri Cartier-Bresson.

Link's Norfolk and Western project was state-of-the art at the time, however, in important ways. His use of a battery-capacitor power supply flash system presaged today's flashguns. And his vision, which developed organically during the course of the project, for what we today would call a multimedia view of the N&W in steam, including photography, sound, and film, was decades ahead of its time.

Just as the railroad and the communities Link photographed have utterly changed, photography has changed so much since the 1950s that any duplication of Link's work is practically impossible. This is due largely to the virtual unavailability of flashbulbs. The light generated by the present-day alternative, flashguns, is so different—at least to this observer's eye—that it would be almost impossible to duplicate Link's results with today's flash equipment. In addition, although it is never likely to completely vanish, film photography has been almost completely replaced by digital photography. Film photography, the medium Link mastered, will become more and more difficult to learn and use in the coming years.

This chapter brings together a number of images to document Link's working method. Plates 153 and 154 are self-portraits taken in the Roanoke N&W passenger station while Link reviewed it as a subject for his photography. As mentioned above, Link spent much of 1955 scouting the N&W for photo locations: These views help document this scouting process.

Link also spent a great deal of time at his New York home base, preparing for his visits to the N&W service area. In New York, he developed his lighting systems, purchased and learned to use tape recorders, held an exhibit at his studio, and started the business of selling his self-published recordings of railroad sounds. Plate 155 is of Link working on a power supply at his workshop in New York, while plate 156 shows Link and his assistant George Thom with his flash system as it fires.

Plates 157 to 166 show Link and some of his assistants in the field: unpacking equipment from the trunk of his car; using a view camera (plates 158, 159, 160, 162, and 165); and posing with a full selection of equipment in the field (plate 166). Although a number of the photos in this book were taken with a Rolleiflex, no photo of Link using this type of camera is available to represent the technical side of this part of the N&W project.

Locations for a number of Link's most noted photographs are shown in the following plates:

- Plate 160 shows a view camera setup at the Gooseneck Dam on the Maury River, Virginia (see plate 113).
- Plate 161 shows a setup to take views at Hager Tower (see plate 33).
- Plate 162 shows one of Link's setups at Hawksbill Creek in Luray, Virginia (see plate 119).
- Plate 163 shows the elaborate setup for *The Lone Star*

Shifter Gets Under Way (NW 1359; see plate 75) and other views at this location.

- Plate 164 shows a setup on the Pope family's porch in Max Meadows, Virginia (see plate 124).

Plates 167 to 175 show Link and his assistants making his well-known sound recordings, a number of which are featured in the disc accompanying this book. This sequence begins with George Thom making the first, unsatisfactory recordings, in March 1956, using an amateur Webcor tape recorder. Plates 168 through 171 show the professional, monaural Tapesonic recorder, often being run by Link's nephew, assistant, and model, Leroy "Corky" Zider III, as well as studies of microphone placements (plates 170 and 171). Plate 172 shows Corky climbing and "fixing the wires."[85] Plate 173 shows sound recording taking place on a train with the Tapesonic; plate 174 shows Link making a recording in the field; and plate 175 shows Link operating the then state-of-the-art stereophonic Ampex tape recorder used for the later recordings in the N&W project.

Plates 176 and 177 show Link's innovative, self-curated *Stop, Look & Listen* exhibit. The people who visited the exhibit are of interest as well: Plate 176 shows Link with friend and N&W engineer Walter Finney, while plate 177 shows Link's assistant George Thom with *Trains* editor David P. Morgan. Model Pat Hall was Link's girlfriend throughout the years of his Norfolk and Western project, and plate 178 gives her a place in the story, showing her posing with Link's first self-produced record album, *Sounds of Steam Railroading*, released in 1957. Plate 179 closes this part of the sequence by depicting Link with his rented Arriflex movie camera.

Link and his assistants enjoyed their visits to Maryland, Virginia, West Virginia, and North Carolina, and plates 180 to 182 show them in the field during downtimes—at a campfire that seems to be a demon reaching out for Link, while eating, and as Zider is warming up with a grizzled railroader. Plate 183 closes the chapter and this book, as Link watches a steam-powered N&W train pass into the night, while the "magnetic flagman" (the automatic wigwag railroad crossing signal) waves a prophetic warning: A fitting end to our look at the Norfolk and Western project of O. Winston Link.

TECHNICAL NOTES

PHOTOGRAPHY

CAMERAS: For posed shots, the Graphic View camera, a 4 x 5 inch view camera, was generally used. Lenses used were usually a $5\frac{1}{4}$-inch normal lens and a $3\frac{5}{8}$-inch wide-angle lens. For more candid shots, Link used a Rolleiflex, a medium-format roll-film camera.

FILM: Link usually used Kodak Super Panchro-Press Type B film, a black-and-white film with an ASA of 100. For color images, Link generally used Ektachrome or Anscochrome, both ASA 24.

LIGHTING: Link used flashbulbs, generally Sylvania Blue Dot bulbs. He used combinations of #2, #0, #25, and #3.

REFLECTORS: Link used commercially available single-flash reflectors, as well as a series of four- to eighteen-bulb reflectors made to his order from spun aluminum.

SYNCHRONIZATION: In order to photograph moving trains, Link usually used synchronized lighting (timing the camera shutter to open as the flashbulbs—or today's flashguns—fire), rather than an open flash, where the shutter is held open and then the lighting fires; this latter method generally cannot operate faster than $\frac{1}{50}$ of a second. Electrical solenoids, synchronized with his lighting system, were used to operate the camera shutters.

LIGHTING SYSTEM: From the beginning of his N&W project through March 1956, Link used flash equipment wired in parallel. Although parallel wiring allows the system to work even if a single bulb is faulty, it requires a great deal of power (up to twelve 6-volt batteries of the time, each weighing about 6 pounds) and does not allow for easy tests of circuit continuity. After some failed photographs, Link invented a battery-capacitor power supply (similar in circuitry, if not weight, to the power supplies for today's flashguns) weighing about 10 pounds. It had three series lighting circuits, each with its own monitoring feature, as well as a circuit that could fire the solenoids of up to three cameras. The disadvantage of the series circuit, of course, was that a fault would break that entire lighting circuit, which then had to be manually checked to find the break.

ASSISTANTS: Link's known assistants for the Norfolk and Western project were George Thom, Leroy "Corky" Zider III, Thomas H. Garver, Denman Zirkle, David Plowden, and Johnny Robertson.[86]

TAPE RECORDINGS

The original recordings resulting from Link's Norfolk and Western project, all self-released, were *Sounds of Steam Railroading* (1957), *The Fading Giant* (1958), *Thunder on Blue Ridge* (1959), *2nd Pigeon and the Mockingbird* (1961), and *Mainline to Panther* (1977). The jacket copy for the first four recordings is attributed to Ben Bane Dulaney; the copy for the final recording was cowritten by noted railfan photographer H. Reid and Norfolk and Western manager Hobart Scott.

Fortunately, Link's recordings postdated the invention of the tape recorder. His first recordings, made on a small, home-use tape recorder, were not successful, due to both the low quality of the equipment and his lack of technical experience with tape recording. The first successful recordings were made on a Tapesonic recorder, a very heavy, durable monophonic tape recorder. At first, Link used house power to operate the recorder, but challenges related to the availability of house power on location led him to develop a power supply, a motor generator providing 120-volt AC current powered by two automotive batteries. Link and his assistants recorded on 1,800-foot reels of tape at 7 1/2 inches per second. Later in the project (beginning in mid-1958), Link purchased a then state-of-the-art Ampex stereophonic tape recorder and largely used this recorder, with the battery power supply, through the end of the project.

Link's steam locomotive recordings are listed in the National Recording Registry of the National Recording Preservation Board and are therefore preserved in the U.S. Library of Congress.[87] All of the *Sounds of Steam Railroading* records (Link's name for the series of recordings as well as the title of the first recording in the group, originally released from 1957 to 1977 as 12-inch, 33 1/3 rpm long-playing records) have been reissued on CD and are currently in print and available for purchase. The CD included with this book is largely composed of the finest of Link's unreleased sound recordings. Many of these were recorded simultaneously with the taking of photographs featured in this book. Liner notes for these exciting, newly released recordings appear on pages 236–37.

For more information about Link's sound recordings, see John Gruber, "O. Winston Link's Sounds of Steam," *Classic Trains* 2:2 (Summer 2001), 22–33; David R. Stephenson, "O. Winston Link's N&W Recordings: More Sounds of Steam Railroading," *The Arrow* 24:1 (January–February–March 2008), 18–24; and Thomas H. Garver, "As Delicate as Air," *Railroad History* 202 (Spring–Summer 2010), 6–13.

MOTION PICTURES

According to Tom Garver's unpublished oral history, "The Thomas H. Garver O. Winston Link Oral History Project," for the small amount of motion picture work that Link did as part of the project, he rented an Arriflex 16mm movie camera with a 200-foot film magazine. He shot a total of about 1,300 feet of color 16mm movie film,

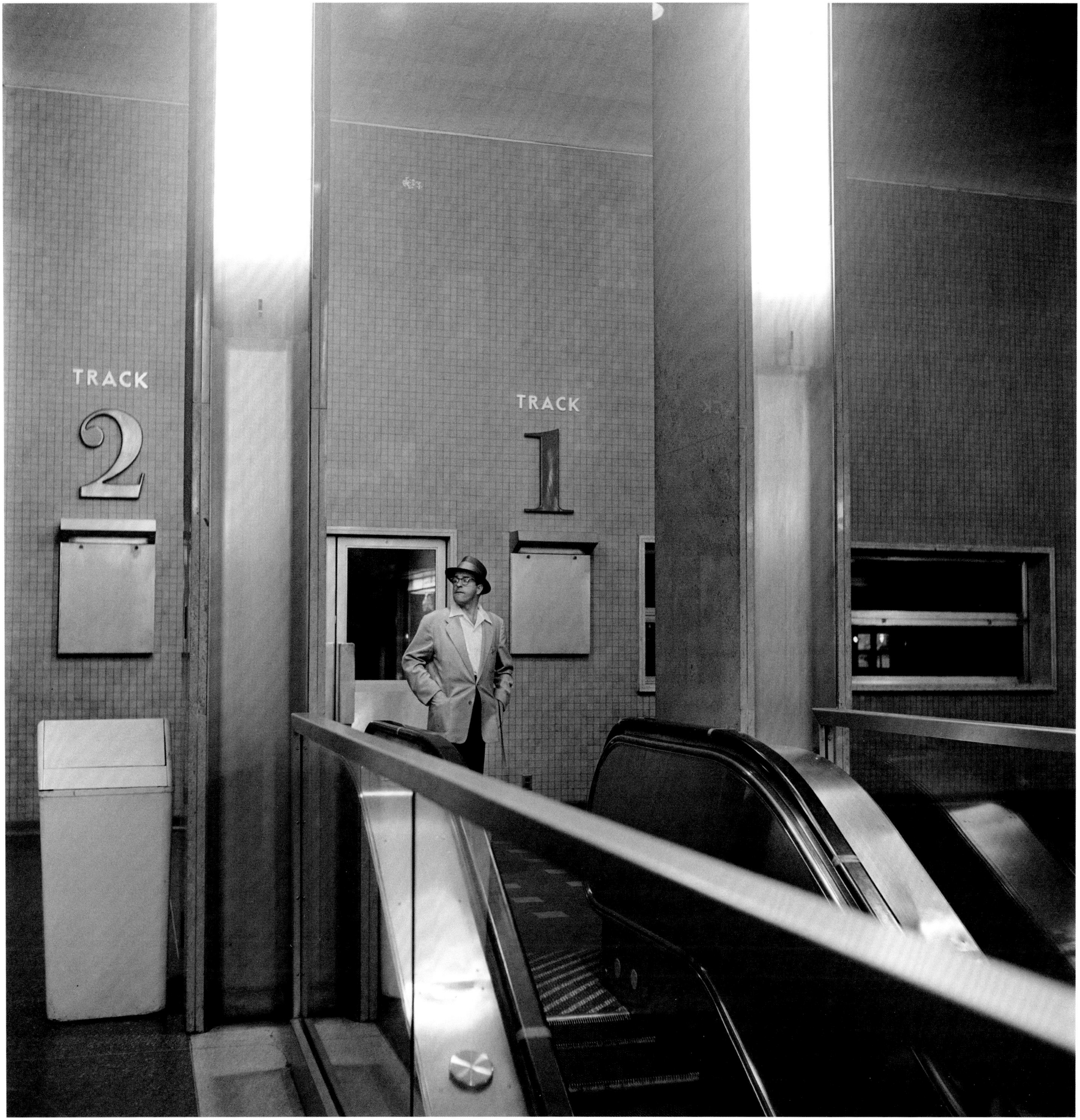
TRACK
2
TRACK
1

PLATE 153   OPPOSITE

**WINSTON LINK ON ESCALATOR DOWN
TO TRACK 1. ROANOKE, VIRGINIA,
JUNE 19, 1955, NW 299**

Over the course of the N&W project, Link started
and ended many trips at the Roanoke passenger
station. Throughout the five years, he made many
photographs in the building and along the line. In
June of 1955, he made a series of self-portraits
late at night. He photographed himself at the
ticket counter (plate 154), on the concourse,
in the waiting area, and, here, at the top of the
escalator, heading to the trackside level.

PLATE 154   RIGHT

**WINSTON LINK AT THE TICKET COUNTER.
ROANOKE, VIRGINIA, JUNE 19, 1955,
NW 301**

To show a customer surrounded by the
modernized décor of the Roanoke station, Link
photographed himself buying a ticket. In this
image, emphasis is given to the illuminated route
map hanging above the ticket counter.

Because Link shot so many images in remote locations, he needed his own power supply. Solving the problem was simple for Link, who made use of his engineering education to create a system that gave him all the energy needed to brightly illuminate any space. Testing the device before risking it on the road was typical of Link's planning.

In 1956, after working on the N&W project for a little over a year, Link held an exhibit of some of the photos in his studio in New York City. The exhibit included a number of the images blown up to a very large size, to show advertising agencies and the art directors of many publications how capable he was of making photos that were very demanding to create. He wished to generate some business—and some interest in the N&W project.

The exhibit, titled *Stop, Look & Listen*, ran from May to September. This photo was the "theme image," and Link (on the left) and his assistant, George Thom, pose with the cameras, large and small flash reflectors, and some of the 4,000 feet of wire needed to make night photos. Also seen are Coleman gas lanterns, and the marker lights Link used to indicate the area in which he had to shoot. His special power supply isn't in the picture (see plate 155). It may not have been completed when this photo was made in early March.

NIGHT EQUIPMENT BEING ASSEMBLED AT LITHIA. LITHIA, VIRGINIA,
DECEMBER 20, 1955, NW 774

A thorough and methodical planner, Link packed his Buick with care for each
trip, knowing he couldn't find replacements for his unique equipment in the
field. Setting up for each shot meant unloading and arranging lights, bulbs,
cords, and cameras. In meticulous fashion, Link numbered his cases in order
to have what he needed for every situation.

WINSTON LINK AND VIEW CAMERA. BOAZ SIDING AT VINTON,
VIRGINIA, APRIL 1959. PHOTO ATTRIBUTED TO DAVID PLOWDEN.
MARCH 1960, NW 2242

When this photograph was taken, Link knew he didn't have much time left
to document steam railroading. This image of him with his 4 x 5 view camera
shows diesel pushers at Bonsack. The water sign and watchman's shack
were seen in several of Link's images, including the cover of his third album,
Thunder on Blue Ridge.

LINK SETS UP TWO VIEW CAMERAS AT BRIDGE 8. WATAUGA, VIRGINIA,
NOVEMBER 1, 1957. PHOTO BY THOMAS H. GARVER, NW 1566

To be certain he captured the image he envisioned, Link often used two
cameras with almost identical, yet slightly different, perspectives. Here,
assistant Tom Garver captured Link as he prepared to make his photograph
Abingdon Branch Mixed Train Crossing Bridge 8 (plate 98).

SETTING UP CAMERA ON THE BANK OF THE MAURY RIVER. BUENA
VISTA, VIRGINIA, MARCH 1, 1956. PHOTO BY GEORGE THOM, NW 973

Considered one of Link's most famous images, *Gooseneck Dam on the Maury
River* (see the variant *Freight Train #88 North at Gooseneck Dam*, plate 113)
was also one of the most labor-intensive. With no bridge across the river at
this location, it took Link a full week to set up the shot and to tear it down.
Using lead lines to carry cords and equipment across, Link's challenge was
to illuminate the tracks across the river in addition to the foreground of rocks
and rushing water, a task made more difficult by the force of the water and
the near-freezing air temperatures.

PLATE 161 LEFT

THE SETUP OF TWO CAMERAS AT HAGER TOWER.
HAGERSTOWN, MARYLAND, MARCH 19, 1956, NW 907

In March 1956, Link set up his gear for two shots at Hager Tower in
Hagerstown. The snow on the ground is evidence of cold weather,
the perfect condition for capturing dramatic plumes of smoke and
steam from a locomotive backing past Hager Tower later that night.
Using two cameras, Link created two different images of the scene,
each with a slight variation in angle and height.

PLATE 162 OPPOSITE

TRAIN #2 NORTHBOUND AT HAWKSBILL CREEK WITH
WINSTON LINK BEHIND THE CAMERA. LURAY, VIRGINIA,
AUGUST 1, 1955, PHOTO ATTRIBUTED TO GEORGE THOM,
NW 369

Link was not afraid to get into the action with his subjects, and
he knew that getting close sometimes meant getting wet. On this
August night, he is testing lighting for one of his most famous
photographs. Not happy with the initial images, he repeated visits
to Hawksbill Creek, making several variants of this photograph
(see plate 119).

PLATE 163 OPPOSITE

LINK ON ROOF PLATFORM AT THE
CLOVERDALE STATION. CLOVERDALE,
VIRGINIA, FEBRUARY 8, 1957, NW 1325

Link's trip of late January to the middle of
February 1957 produced a number of well-
known photos, including *The Lone Star Shifter
Gets Under Way* (plate 75). In order to look down
on the locomotive with the station semaphores
standing proudly in the foreground, Link had to
build this wooden platform on the station's roof,
a vantage point from which he worked during a
long rainy night.

Link laughed and shook his head "no"
when asked, years after making the photo, if
he had patched the holes he made in the roof.
By then, the station, which was once located
on the N&W's Shenandoah Division, had been
demolished for years.

PLATE 164 RIGHT

LINK SETTING UP FOR THE POPES AT
MAX MEADOWS. MAX MEADOWS, VIRGINIA,
PROBABLY DECEMBER 31, 1957, NW 1747

Link loved the porch at the Popes' house in Max
Meadows for the intricate carving and turning.
He was equally impressed with the work it would
take to scrape and paint it. Posing Mr. and Mrs.
Benjamin Pope on their porch as they watched
the last steam-powered passenger train pass,
eastbound, made for some challenging lighting
and a labor-intensive setup. Link's reflectors
were custom-built and made in various sizes to
accommodate this particular space and location.

PLATE 165 PREVIOUS SPREAD, LEFT

LINK SETUP FOR PHOTOGRAPH OF TRAIN #201,
LANSING, NORTH CAROLINA, OCTOBER 1957,
PHOTO BY THOMAS H. GARVER, NW 1453

On a steep bank overlooking the tracks from Lansing, Link is
setting up two view cameras to capture Train #201, moving
south. Creating a slight difference in angle and perspective,
Link often used two cameras to capture a single scene.

PLATE 166 PREVIOUS SPREAD, RIGHT

NIGHT SHOT OF GEORGE THOM WITH BOBBY GOGGIN,
LITHIA, VIRGINIA, DECEMBER 1955, NW 755

In addition to documenting the Norfolk and Western, Link also
documented his effort, and captured images of his setup,
equipment, and assistants. Here he has photographed his
camera, some lighting gear, and his assistant George Thom,
along with Bobby Goggin, a young man he met near Fringer's
Mill in Virginia.

PLATE 167 LEFT

GEORGE THOM RECORDING CROSSING SOUNDS,
LURAY, VIRGINIA, MARCH 23, 1956, NW 834

Always documenting his work, Link photographed the process
of making audio recordings. George Thom is studiously
monitoring the Webcor recorder while making recordings
of the crossing at Luray. Link and Thom have mounted the
microphone on an independent stand, above the ground.

PLATE 168 OPPOSITE

CORKY ZIDER AND TWO DOGS AT THE WYTHEVILLE
STATION, WYTHEVILLE, VIRGINIA, DECEMBER 1957,
NW 1693

Only a few of Link's well-known images from the Norfolk
and Western project contain local dogs, but many of his
behind-the-scenes and variant images do. In Wytheville,
Leroy "Corky" Zider, Link's nephew and assistant, is making
recordings of the passing trains, accompanied by two rather
bedraggled companions.

PLATE 169 OPPOSITE

PLATE 169 OPPOSITE

CORKY ZIDER RECORDING FROM THE TRUNK OF THE BUICK.
SHENANDOAH JUNCTION, WEST VIRGINIA, JANUARY 28, 1957.
NW 1314

Setting up the recording gear in the trunk of the Buick, Corky Zider makes
audio recordings at Shenandoah Junction. In the background, a GP-9
passes by Link's camera and tripod, which are covered with a dark cloth.

PLATE 170 RIGHT

READY TO RECORD. BLUE RIDGE, VIRGINIA, LATE OCTOBER
1957. NW 1541

Carrying his audio recording equipment in his 1952 Buick allowed Link to
be ready to record at a moment's notice. Near Blue Ridge Grade, Link set
up his equipment to record a passing train. A curious dog is caught in the
act of inspecting the equipment.

PLATE 171 OVERLEAF, LEFT

RECORDING EQUIPMENT TO CAPTURE LOCOMOTIVE
INSPECTION. ROANOKE, VIRGINIA, AUGUST 1956. NW 1160

As the N&W project continued, Link became more involved in
documenting the sounds of the railroad as well. With a microphone
on a stand adjacent to the Class J, Link is recording the sounds of an
inspection at the Roanoke station.

PLATE 172 OVERLEAF, RIGHT

CORKY ZIDER ON A SIGNAL BRIDGE. MAX MEADOWS, VIRGINIA.
DECEMBER 1957. NW 1683

During his often physically demanding project, Link was not deterred by
any obstacle from getting the photograph he wanted. Sending Corky
Zider, his nephew and assistant, up a signal mast in Max Meadows was
certainly not uncommon. Many images of Max Meadows were made from
this vantage point.

PLATE 173 PREVIOUS SPREAD, LEFT

RECORDING IN THE LOCOMOTIVE. BLUE RIDGE, VIRGINIA,
MARCH 1958, NW 1826

Looking dapper in a trainman's cap and a summer shirt, Link has set
up his recording equipment in the cab of a Class Y-6, along Blue Ridge
Grade. Under the watchful eyes of a young trainman, Link is intent on
the sounds and machinery.

PLATE 174 PREVIOUS SPREAD, RIGHT

LINK WITH TAPE RECORDER. VINTON, VIRGINIA, JUNE 1958.
PHOTO BY THOMAS H. GARVER, NW 1849

Hidden among the weeds, but with his recording microphone high
above, Link is listening carefully as a pusher passes by Boaz Siding, in
Vinton. Blue Ridge Grade was a challenge for most trains carrying coal,
so a pusher locomotive was often employed to assist. The sounds of a
hardworking locomotive were irresistible to Link.

PLATE 175 LEFT

LINK OPERATING AMPEX ON THE FLOOR OF A BAGGAGE CAR.
WILLIAMSON, WEST VIRGINIA, DECEMBER 24, 1958. PHOTO BY
CORKY ZIDER, NW 2040

With the same meticulous attention he gave to his photographs, Link
made hours of audio recordings, knowing the sounds were just as
precious as the images. Here, he is in mid-recording, with his equipment
spread all over the floor of the baggage car. The sound captured was of
Train #15 arriving in Williamson.

PLATE 176 OPPOSITE

WALTER FINNEY WITH WINSTON LINK EXAMINING A RAILROAD
MARKER LAMP. NEW YORK, NEW YORK, JUNE 1, 1956, PHOTO
BY GEORGE THOM, NW 1053

In 1956, Link held an exhibit of his N&W work, titled *Stop, Look & Listen*.
It ran for the duration of the summer and brought many of Link's friends
and subjects to New York. This was the first exhibit of the work, and in
addition to his photographs, it featured his audio recordings, offering a
multisensory experience of the N&W. Walter Finney was the engineer of
Train #1 and #2, which ran next to Gooseneck Dam on the Maury River.

PLATE 177 PREVIOUS SPREAD, LEFT

DAVE MORGAN AND GEORGE THOM LOOKING AT THE EXHIBIT.
NEW YORK, NEW YORK, JULY 13, 1956, NW 1062

Stop, Look & Listen also caught the eye of the premier railfan
publication, *Trains*. Here, Link's assistant George Thom, on the right,
discusses the work with David P. Morgan, editor of the magazine. Link's
longtime friend and colleague Salem Tamer designed the exhibit, and
all printing was done by a nearby custom-printing lab.

PLATE 178 PREVIOUS SPREAD, RIGHT

PAT HALL POSING WITH *SOUNDS OF STEAM RAILROADING*.
NEW YORK, NEW YORK, MARCH 4, 1958, NW 1797

Model Pat Hall, Link's longtime girlfriend, poses with the first volume of
audio recordings. This photo was probably taken soon after the release
of the LP. Link made a series of images with Hall and the album cover.

PLATE 179 OPPOSITE

LINK WITH MOVIE CAMERA, PHOTOGRAPHER UNKNOWN

During his N&W project, Link made about thirty minutes of 16mm
movie footage. This small part of the project was done as steam was
vanishing, to document the last days. Working in film was certainly not
a natural thing for Link, but the medium gave him the opportunity to
capture the feel of riding the rails from every angle.

PLATE 180 RIGHT

LINK ADDING FUEL TO THE FIRE. FRINGER'S MILL, VIRGINIA,
DECEMBER 1955, PHOTO BY GEORGE THOM, NW 768

Cold winter air produced dramatic steam and smoke from steam
locomotives. Darkness allowed Link to emphasize elements of a scene,
selectively using light he provided. But shooting at night during the
winter often made this process more challenging and less comfortable.
In this case, Link and assistant George Thom have built a fire and take
turns sitting by it, while waiting for the train to arrive.

PLATE 181 TOP

LINK AND CORKY ZIDER EATING A MEAL. MAX MEADOWS,
VIRGINIA, DECEMBER 1957, PHOTOGRAPHER UNKNOWN,
NW 1719

Since so many of Link's images were imagined and created in
darkness, the project often involved late nights and waiting in cold
environs. Given his close relationship with many station agents and
crews along the line, Link was occasionally able to seek shelter
and warmth inside a station. Here, he and his assistant Corky Zider
take a break to eat at the Max Meadows station.

PLATE 182 BOTTOM

CORKY ZIDER STANDING IN THE SHENANDOAH JUNCTION
STATION WARMING HIS HANDS. SHENANDOAH JUNCTION,
WEST VIRGINIA, JANUARY 30, 1957, NW 1316

Long days outside in the cold, while shooting and recording, made
it hard to stay warm. At Shenandoah Junction, an N&W employee
and Corky Zider try to warm up at a stove that has certainly seen
some use through the years.

PLATE 183 OPPOSITE

WINSTON LINK AND A PASSING TRAIN. PANTHER,
WEST VIRGINIA, AUGUST 1958, NW 1994

Link was often drawn to placing large objects in the foreground
of his photographs. Crouched below a magnetic flagman, Link
watches a train moving away.

AFTERWORD
BY CONWAY LINK

"All aboard!" The woman and her son walked over to a waiting passenger car, climbed the steps, and found their seats. The steam locomotive, soon to be replaced by a diesel, got a few more coals shoveled into the firebox, the whistle blew, and the passenger train pulled out of the station. For the woman, my mother, it was the last farewell—the final departure from New York. She never returned.

I didn't grow up around my dad. Most of what I knew about him and his side of the family, when I was a child, I learned from my mother and my mother's mother. At Christmastime and birthdays, presents would arrive from New York. The steam locomotive sets are still some of my most prized possessions from childhood—one, a 0-4-0, #1656, and another, a 6-8-6, #671. On each he affixed one of his "OWL" stickers, usually in a hard-to-see place—perhaps to escape the eyes of my mother.

It wasn't until I was twelve that I saw him again. Cards came with regularity until I was sixteen, at which time I received the last birthday card. "Come to New York. I have something in the works" was the message. I didn't reply for fear of getting my mother stirred up.

For the next five years there was no contact. Then it was I who initiated it. Prodded by my mother's mother, who had some favorable memories of Dad, I wrote to him. He responded. Things changed. Within a week, I began receiving copies of family information; some arrived in red or green mailing envelopes (not the usual manila variety), with commemorative stamps, the top and right-hand edges affixed equidistant from the edges of the envelope. Rubber-stamped with PHOTOGRAPHS, DO NOT BEND and other instructions, these envelopes were created with careful thought.

As an adult, I was invited with my wife, Marilyn, to the "ancestral home" at 483 Eighth Street in Brooklyn. Even though I spent time there as a child, I had almost no recollection of the four-story brownstone. OWL's favorite greasy spoon, "Roach Haven," at the corner of Eighth Avenue and Ninth Street, was where I received my first lesson of Link Family Humor 101. At the counter, a patron was smoking a cigar next to OWL. The cigar smoker got up to use the restroom, and Link went to work, dousing the lit cigar in a glass of water, then returning the unlightable cigar to the ashtray. Upon his return, thinking the cigar went out on its own, the man went through a complete book of matches trying to get it going again, but to no avail. This was just the beginning of my exposure to Link's practical jokes.

It was during time spent in the basement of 483 that I learned more about my dad. The basement was a treasure trove of neat old stuff. There was his workbench, made by his father in 1915. Stored in a drawer in the bench was the silver Link seal that Hans Jacob Linck (John Jacob Link), of Grossgartach, Germany, brought with him when he immigrated to the colonies in 1733. There was the typewriter Dad had used for at least thirty years, the cot he sometimes slept on, railroad lanterns, switch lamps, locomotive builder's plates, an early wire-type recording unit, and lots of mysterious storage boxes.

We talked photography and cameras, but not enough. Long before the reconnection, I had splurged for a used Ricoh 35mm rangefinder. It performed satisfactorily, but I talked my dad into financing a "real" 35mm SLR, a Miranda Sensorex, and a pair of "high-quality" Vivitar T-4 lenses. It was only after camera number three, a Canon FTb, that I began to take photography more seriously.

Dad dropped by our home in 1971 to see his new granddaughter. We then met in Fort Smith, Arkansas, in 1974; in Magnolia, Arkansas, with a side trip to the Reader Railroad, in 1975; and in Alexandria, Louisiana, in 1977, for a meeting of great importance. Good advice ("Keep busy") is what he offered that November afternoon when he learned a divorce was in the works. My daughter's spirits were lifted considerably by her grandfather's shenanigans.

Two years went by until the next visit, when my daughter and I picked up Amtrak in Marshall, Texas, and were dropped off at Penn Station about thirty-eight hours later. The meetings after that took place in Louisiana. With his work in Texas or south Louisiana, my house was a convenient spot for him to stay. I cooked; he ate. The proportion of time devoted to photography discussions increased. He was aware that I had won or placed in several local photo contests, and in recognition of this new direction I was taking, he wrote in my 1980 Museum of Modern Art appointment calendar a powerful confidence-building comment: "Conway—At the rate you are going with your photography, you will soon excel me. You are doing great. Dad." His elevated opinion of my limited successes was the basis for his asking my opinion on which of the N&W images should be included in his first book, *Steam, Steel & Stars*, which was in the beginning stages in those days. We spent many hours poring over N&W contact prints, which were spread out across the top of the vintage oak round kitchen table.

The last time I saw my dad in Brooklyn was in August 1983. At the brownstone, my daughter had finished mowing the postage-stamp back lawn with a push mower, when she asked if she could water the flower bed. Dad ran a hose through the kitchen window and attached it to the kitchen faucet. The watering went well at first.

Link never left the sink, however, and slowly began shutting off the water. Anne responded by examining the end of the hose to determine if there was a water-blocking obstruction. OWL yelled out the kitchen window, "You're holding it too tight!" and simultaneously rotated the handle, dousing his granddaughter, who took it all in fun and still laughs about it today.

Dad was different on this visit—much busier. His work was being noticed, and he had an important interview with a reporter for the London *Times*, so our time with him was limited. However, we all attended the opening of *Ghost Trains: Railroad Photographs of the 1950s by O. Winston Link* at the International Center of Photography in Manhattan—which was quite an adventure. Dad was pleased at the reception and that his granddaughter was in attendance.

In the past he had been almost 100 percent attentive, especially to his granddaughter. Now he appeared distracted, and in retrospect, he was probably involved with Conchita Mendoza, the future Mrs. O. Winston Link #2, whom he married just a short time later. From 1983 to 1992, the new Mrs. Link separated her husband from friends and relatives alike. The damage done to our relationship was almost irreparable. Letters were not answered. Christmas, birthday, and Father's Day gifts went unacknowledged. Rarely was it possible to bypass this self-appointed censor.

Link had seen it coming—the marital problems had escalated to the first magnitude or even greater. He removed the N&W negatives from his home one evening and entrusted them to his good friend Scott MacPhee. The negatives were stored at Scott's house until Link could return and place them in a safe-deposit box. Shortly thereafter, Mrs. Link put chains on the spiral staircase to block access to the upper level of their house, changed the exterior door locks, and removed the wheels and coil wire from his Model A. In February 1992, the drought of our separation ended with a telephone call. My dad, freed from his bastille, gave me a brief description of the most recent and important events.

Conchita and her boyfriend had not only robbed my dad of some of his best photographs, significant negatives, furniture, tools, locomotive builder's plates, locomotive parts, valuable stamp collections, medicine, fifteen original Currier and Ives prints, cameras, enlargers, exhibition catalogs, and family heirlooms, but pilfered some of his winter clothing as well. Before the courts returned his house to him, he lived in his car, stayed with friends, or rented a motel room in Brewster, New York.

For our first meeting after a forced nine-year separation, we met him at the Brickyard, a local watering hole in Danbury, Connecticut, which doubled as an eatery. The stress of the marriage to Conchita, health issues, and the loss of almost everything he owned had taken its toll. We didn't pick up where we left off in 1983. Everyone had to do a bit of adjusting to one another's life experiences. Meetings took place at his good friend Scott MacPhee's. Over the next week, I realized that although he had taken quite a hit, he was determined to recover from his adversity, with the primary focus on obtaining a divorce. He was determined to rebuild his life.

More "red letter" days followed: In November 1993, a big exhibit opened in New Orleans, at A Gallery for Fine Photography on Royale Street. Dad was on hand for three days, greeting Link enthusiasts and signing *Steam, Steel & Stars* and a large stack of *Ghost Trains* (a 1983 Chrysler Museum publication purchased by gallery owner Joshua Mann Pailet). His portable audience—

friend Joan Thomas; granddaughter Anne; her fiancé, Jay; my friend Cindy; and myself—enjoyed his serious side during the television and radio interviews, but loved his outrageous humor during the several days of book signing. A vice-chancellor of the university where I taught made the trek and was about to have her book signed. Link asked what she wanted him to write. She turned to me and said, "Conway, what should he write?" That's what he wrote.

Link was addicted to live steam, and in August 1997, the New Hope and Ivyland Railroad in New Hope, Pennsylvania, called our names. A drive from Connecticut to Pennsylvania for a steam ride wouldn't be on most potential adventure lists. But then again, Link made his own list and rules. It was a rare opportunity to ride in the cab with him shooting video with one hand, taking stills with the second hand, and using my third hand to stabilize.

The other big event of the year took place at Link's South Salem house in New York. Beginning in the late morning, he asked for help with what he had salvaged of his non-N&W negatives. For hours on end we sat side by side, with him taking out bundle after bundle of negatives, removing a few samples from each bundle, and deciding on "what to leave in and what to leave out." At the end of the day, Link had filled a rather large bag of discards. I asked if I could take them with me back to Louisiana, and he said, "Sure, there may be something in there you can use." It would be six years before I went through the almost-destroyed images.

The telephone rang in late March the next year. Dad asked how quickly we could get to Tennessee. A new adventure was in the works, and he needed help getting around. He would be in Harriman, Tennessee, for the filming of some of the scenes of

October Sky. We were there in two days. Even though the movie was released in early 1999, it wasn't until May that he saw it for the first time, when we took him to Watertown, Connecticut. He loved it. It was about America. It was about space. He loved both.

In my youth, my mother was not forthcoming with information about me to my dad and did not permit visits. OWL resorted to ingenious information-gathering tactics. I began to discover this after a call from Fritz Williams, a childhood chum with whom I had not been in contact since elementary school, who laid out quite a tale. Unbeknownst to me, it seems my father would come to town and stay with the Williams family, pretending to be an uncle, so that he would be able to see me when I came over. Then there were the documents and letters—correspondence between my father and the principal of a school I attended—whereby my dad was able to drop in and take photos, which offered another opportunity for a brief encounter. Photos taken back in those days, and not recognized by my mother or me, confirm this. Correspondence with Dad's sister showed his intention of my being taken care of in the case of his untimely demise, even down to which colleges he did not want me to attend.

Eventually the rapprochement of my parents took place—beginning slowly, at a snail's pace, initiated by my father after our reconnection. Clearly, the Conchita-induced dark ages (1983–1992) were not conducive to such camaraderie, but by February 1993, my long-divorced parents were corresponding again. In July 1997, while waiting outside the Martha Washington Inn in Abingdon, Virginia, Dad said, "I don't know what happened in the mar-

riage to your mother. I don't know why it didn't work. The war was going on and I had to work late into the night." That comment gave me hope that they would get together at least once. Maybe in New Orleans, where my mother had been his model in some of those great French Quarter images sixty years earlier, in 1937, when she was nineteen, and he was five years older. Just once more. I think they both wanted to. It didn't happen.

The last time we saw Dad alive was in August 2000 in New York. The funeral at the family plot in West Virginia was attended by Joan Thomas, my daughter Anne, my friend Cindy, a smattering of Dad's friends, and a small group from Virginia. That Virginia contingent represented visionary folks in Roanoke who wished to create a first-class museum to showcase Link's N&W photography. Three years later, in January 2004, the O. Winston Link Museum opened in the updated Norfolk and Western Railway station, near the Hotel Roanoke, the Virginia Museum of Transportation, and other historic properties in the downtown area. The Museum is a remarkable tribute to my father.

The work my father created captures American life at mid-century, and this book intends to show that vision beyond the images we already know and love. My father was passionate and dedicated, qualities that I hope are visible in the images included here. He showed his love for me and for his work with tireless perseverance. There were adventures and laughter and devotion in every part of his life, a lesson that I still try to learn from today.

Shreveport, Louisiana, 2011

NOTES

1 When an N&W photo is discussed in this book, the specific "NW" negative number is provided, so that interested scholars can refer to the exact photo being mentioned. Link's Norfolk and Western project is often referred to as the "NW project" as a result of the numbering system Link used for his negatives.

2 Richard Saunders Jr., *Merging Lines* (DeKalb: Northern Illinois University Press, 2001), 103.

3 For a survey of Richard Steinheimer's work, see Richard Steinheimer and Jeff Brouws, *A Passion for Trains: The Railroad Photography of Richard Steinheimer* (New York: W. W. Norton and Company, 2004). A survey of Jim Shaughnessy's work is cited elsewhere in the text. A survey of Philip R. Hastings's photography awaits an author.

4 Facts about Link's parents and siblings, and life, are largely from Thomas H. Garver, *O. Winston Link: The Man and the Museum* (Roanoke, Virginia: O. Winston Link Museum, 2004), 3. The information given in this book sometimes differs from that in Link and Garver's *The Last Steam Railroad in America*, cited below. This author has tried to avoid including possible inaccuracies. The recent release of Albert Link Jr.'s self-published *O. Winston Link: A Family Album* (Mahopac, New York: TC Graphics, 2009) has provided new information, making facts about Link's parents clearer and more accessible.

5 See Albert Link Jr., *O. Winston Link: A Family Album*, for details of Link's education.

6 Garver, *O. Winston Link: The Man and the Museum*, 3.

7 O. Winston Link, photographs; text by Thomas H. Garver, *The Last Steam Railroad in America* (New York: Harry N. Abrams, Inc., 1995), 136.

8 For a book-length review of the work of one of Link's contemporaries in this field, see Tim B. Wride, *Retail Fictions: The Commercial Photography of Ralph Bartholomew Jr.* (Los Angeles: Los Angeles County Museum of Art, 1998). For a general overview of advertising photography, both in Link's period and beyond, see Robert A. Sobieszek, *The Art of Persuasion* (New York: Harry N. Abrams, Inc., 1988).

9 See Conway Link's Louisiana Link website, http://louisianalink.net.

10 Garver, *O. Winston Link: The Man and the Museum*, 4; also http://louisianalink.net/bio.html.

11 See http://www.louisianalink.net/bio.html.

12 Garver, *O. Winston Link: The Man and the Museum*, 5.

13 For examples, see Link and Garver, *The Last Steam Railroad in America*, 137.

14 For a small but interesting portfolio of them, see Kevin P. Keefe, "Link Where You'd Least Expect Him," *Trains* 61:6 (June 2001): 42–49. The article was put together from prints that Link submitted to *Trains* editor David P. Morgan in the 1950s. It is also known that Link undertook commercial photography for the Pennsylvania Railroad.

15 Details of Link's life during this period are from Link and Garver, *The Last Steam Railroad in America*, 142.

16 The only known surviving item of correspondence between Link and the *Trains* staff is a letter from Link to editor David P. Morgan, dated October 16, 1956.

17 Thomas H. Garver, "Travelling Light," *Practical Photography* (May 1996): 85.

18 Link identifies the man as Troy Humphries, later featured in a number of Link's photographs, in his unpublished poem "The Rose on the Table" (1960).

19 Details of the evening are from O. Winston Link, photographs; text by Tim Hensley, afterword by Thomas H. Garver, *Steam, Steel & Stars: America's Last Steam Railroad* (New York: Harry N. Abrams, Inc., 1987), 11.

20 Tony Reevy, telephone interview with Thomas H. Garver, September 2003. (All Reevy interviews noted here were conducted in writing Reevy's 2004 article, "Print & Image: O. Winston Link," in *Railroad History* 190 [Spring–Summer 2004]: 78–99.)

21 As quoted in Link and Hensley, *Steam, Steel & Stars*, 12.

22 Link and Garver, *The Last Steam Railroad in America*, 32.

23 Link and Hensley, *Steam, Steel & Stars*, 129.

24 Garver, *O. Winston Link: The Man and the Museum*, 7.

25 Thomas H. Garver has prepared an unpublished listing of Link's Norfolk and Western project field trips, "O. Winston Link: Details of His Trips to the Norfolk and Western Railway, Taken from his Notebooks and Negative Files," (2003, 2007). Another critical, unpublished resource maintained by Garver is Link's résumé, which includes books and exhibition catalogs, articles, selected reproductions, television programs, sound recordings, an exhibition history, and selected public and corporate collections.

26 "The Mixed Train" (daytime views of the Abingdon Branch), pages 31–43, in the July 1957 issue, and "Steam After Dark" (a portfolio of N&W night photos taken as of that time), pages 30–43, in the November 1957 issue. Text in both articles is not by Link, who rarely wrote copy; it is attributed to David P. Morgan.

27 *Trains,* 17:5 (March 1957): 44.

28 Thomas H. Garver, "As Delicate as Air," *Railroad History* 202 (Spring–Summer 2010): 8. A photo published in a period *Trains* shows Morgan at the exhibit (see *Trains* 18:9 [July 1958]: 10), as do NW 1062, 1063, and 1064; photos NW 1053–1061 show Finney at the exhibit.

29 Allan Ripp, "Night Tricks," *American Photographer* 8:6 (June 1982): 50.

30 According to Garver's unpublished listing of Link's field trips to visit the N&W (see note 25).

31 Jeffrey W. Schramm, *Out of Steam: Dieselization and American Railroads, 1920–1960* (Bethlehem, Pennsylvania: Lehigh University Press, 2010), 200.

32 See http://www.newyorktrains.com/projects.htm.

33 Garver, *O. Winston Link: The Man and the Museum*, 33–34.

34 Jim Boyd, "The O. Winston Link Museum," *Railfan & Railroad* 22:10 (October 2003): 62.

35 They are, as best as can be determined through comparing the museum record with the N&W photographs, NW 362, NW 720, NW 792, NW 1103 (actually a photomontage), and NW 1648. At the same time as the purchase, Link donated a print of NW 1230. These are the only Link photo-graphs MoMA owns to date. Unfortunately, they are not listed on MoMA's online listing of collections; those interested must contact the museum for a list. They are cataloged at MoMA as 274.1976, 271.1976, 275.1976, 340.1976, 272.1976, and 273.1976.

36 Daniel Machalabra, "Fame Arrives Late for a Photographer of Trains at Night – O. Winston Link, 71, an Artist of the Late Steam Age, Is Acclaimed as a Virtuoso," *Wall Street Journal* (January 13, 1986; Eastern edition): 1.

37 David Plowden's breakout had occurred earlier, but it was not as a result of his railroad-subject photography; his first major book of railroad-subject images, *A Time of Trains* (New York: W. W. Norton and Company), was published in 1987. Plowden's most recent book features railroad-subject photographs: *Requiem for Steam: The Railroad Photographs of David Plowden* (New York: W. W. Norton Company, 2010).

38 Tony Reevy, telephone interview with Bill Johnson, October 5, 2003.

39 Kathy Field Stephen, "Mr. Link Hails the Train," *Christian Science Monitor* (September 19, 1983; The Home Forum section): 20.

40 Critics have often used Frank as an example of Link's creative opposite. However, there are obvious affinities between their bodies of work in terms of subject—similarities that have perhaps been cloaked by the differences in their technical methods of photography. Compare, for example, Link's well-known *Hotshot Eastbound* (NW 1103; see page 22), with *Drive-in movie—Detroit*, on page 101 of Robert Frank's *The Americans* (New York: Grove Press, 1959). Note that titles of Link's photos often differ slightly among sources; the author has generally used the title found in the records at the O. Winston Link Museum.

41 Interview in Tony Reevy, "Print and Image: O. Winston Link," *Railroad History* 190 (Spring–Summer 2004): 89–90.

42 Reevy, telephone interview with Garver, September 2003.

43 Reevy, telephone interview with Johnson, October 5, 2003.

44 See Robin Updike, "Tracing a Love Affair with Locomotives—Photographs of Trains Represent America's Never-Sated Wanderlust," *The Seattle Times* (July 27, 1997; Sunday Final Edition): L7; Arturo Silva, "Two Moments of Genius," *The Daily Yomiuri* (August 6, 1993): 15.

45 Reevy, telephone interview with Garver, September 2003.

46 Andy Grundberg, "Photography View: Documents of the Steam Train That Approach the Surreal," *The New York Times* (September 4, 1983): 20H.

47 The heading is from Barry Meier, "A Fairy-Tale Ending Derailed," *The New York Times* (April 3, 1994): Section 2, 1.

48 Garver, *O. Winston Link: The Man and the Museum*, 37.

49 Paul Yule's documentary *The Photographer, His Wife, Her Lover* (Berwick Universal Pictures, 2006; color) reviews this controversy in detail.

50 See Garver's unpublished oral history of O. Winston Link, "The Thomas H. Garver O. Winston Link Oral History Project," for more details about Link and Thomas.

51 Garver, *O. Winston Link: The Man and the Museum*, 37.

52 According to Garver in his unpublished oral history, "The Thomas H. Garver O. Winston Link Oral History Project."

53 Link stated he liked the work of Diane Arbus, but also stated he only learned of her work in the early 1980s; see Andrew Stephen, "Closely Observed Trains," *Sunday Times Magazine* (June 19, 1983): 36.

54 See John Raeburn, *A Staggering Revolution: A Cultural History of Thirties Photography* (Chicago: University of Illinois Press, 2006).

55 The FSA was originally called the Resettlement Administration.

56 For background on Evans's work for *Fortune*, see Lesley K. Baier's *Walker Evans at 'Fortune' 1945–1965* (Wellesley, Mass.: Wellesley College Museum, 1977); Gilles Mora and John T. Hill's *Walker Evans: The Hungry Eye* (New York: Harry N. Abrams, Inc., 1993); and, most recently, Anne M. Lyden's *Railroad Vision: Photography, Travel, and Perception* (Los Angeles: The J. Paul Getty Museum, 2003), which featured five Evans photos, three of which were not among his well-known images. The book also features four images by Link, whose work is discussed on pages 118–20.

57 These are "Along the Right-of-Way" (September 1950, 106–13); "The U.S. Depot" (February 1953, 138–43), "Before They Disappear" (March 1957, 141–45), and "The Last of Railroad Steam" (September 1958, 137–41).

58 Compare, for example, *Peace Among the Cinders,* on page 141 of this portfolio, with Link's *Jimbo, "The Hound of Husk"* (NW 1506).

59 Interestingly, Robert Frank was also a protégé of Evans, and Evans placed Frank's portfolio focusing on a Pennsylvania Railroad train, the "Congressional" [officially, "The Morning Congressional" and "The Afternoon Congressional"] in *Fortune* (November 1955): 118–22. A view similar to the photograph that opened "The Congressional" appears in Frank's *The Americans* (New York: Grove Press, 1959), 25. *The Americans* joined Evans's *Walker Evans: American Photographs* (New York: Museum of Modern Art, 1938) as one of the most influential photography books of the twentieth century, and became the standard work for Frank's followers in the street photography movement.

60 Garver's unpublished oral history, "The Thomas H. Garver O. Winston Link Oral History Project," contains a full discussion of Garver's view of Link's influences.

61 Compare Link's *Interior of the Station at Waynesboro, Virginia* (NW 3) with Hastings's photo on page 100 of Jeff Brouws and Ed Delvers, *Starlight on the Rails* (New York: Harry N. Abrams, Inc., 2000), both taken in 1955; also compare Shaughnessy's *Norfolk & Western Y-6b 2-8-8-2 #2129 and Helper Crew, Boaz Siding, Near Vinton, Virginia, 1957*—plate 81 in Jeff Brouws (text) and Jim Shaughnessy (photographs), *The Call of Trains: Railroad Photographs by Jim Shaughnessy* (New York: W. W. Norton & Company, 2008)—with Link's *Class A, Lanterns and Funnels* (NW 2132) and *Highball for the Doubleheader* (NW 2127).

62 Tony Reevy, telephone interview with Steve Barry, August 29, 2003.

63 *Rutland Freight Train with RS3 #206 on High Bridge Across Walloomsac River, North Hoosick, New York, 1959* (plate 57 in *The Call of Trains*) and *Rutland Freight Train RC-2 with RS3 #208 on Bridge Over Walloomsac River Near State Line, New York, 1959* (plate 101 in *The Call of Trains*).

64 This movement is exemplified by icons of today's art photography world such as Laurie Simmons (born 1949). It is largely an outgrowth of the Conceptual Art movement of the 1960s and '70s, which is exemplified by photographers and artists such as Eleanor Antin (born 1935), but Link is also an obvious influence on the constructed reality photographers.

65 See http://www.artcat.com/exhibits/12846 and http://www.artnet.com/galleries/Exhibitions.asp?gid=117084&cid=129091.

66 For a survey of Wall's work, see Rolf Lauter, ed., *Jeff Wall: Figures and Places—Selected Works from 1978–2000* (Munich: Prestel, 2001). *Eviction Struggle* appears there as plate 25. *The Drain* appears on page 161 of Diarmuid Costello and Margaret Iversen, eds., *Photography After Conceptual Art* (Chichester, England: Wiley-Blackwell, 2010).

67 See http://www.calcego.com/en/obra.asp?ref=GC&num=0003.

68 For more about Crewdson and his work, see http://www.whitecube.com/artists/crewdson. A number of books are also available.

69 For the best published examples, see Lucius Beebe, *High Iron* (New York: D. Appleton-Century Company, 1938).

70 "Speeders" are small motorized four-wheel track-inspection cars, and automotive "hi-railers" are automobiles, usually pickup trucks, modified with retractable railroad wheels so that they can drive on roads or railroad tracks.

71 Branch lines are lines that split off from main lines, usually terminating in small or medium-size towns. Secondary main lines have less traffic than nearby competitors, usually because they were built later and/or not located as strategically.

72 Railroad employment is very complex, and usage of terms such as trainman, brakeman, and flagman varied regionally, and from company to company. Train-crew employees working in yards had conductors or foremen and switchmen, a position related to the position of brakeman, but in a yard service track of employment; on-line trainmen were generally conductors and brakemen; usage sometimes varied between passenger- and freight-train crews. On-line engine crews were composed of engineers and firemen. See http://www.bls.gov/oco/ocos244.htm for an overview of railroad employment today. For definitions of positions such as flagman, fireman, baggageman, head-end brakeman, rear-end brakeman, etc., historical sources, such as *A Treasury of Railroad Folklore* (see below), must also be consulted.

73 For details of N&W steam locomotives and steam locomotive rosters, see Richard E. Prince, *Norfolk & Western Railway: Pocahontas Coal Carrier* (Millard, Nebraska: Richard E. Prince, 1980). Also useful is Lewis Ingles Jeffries, *N&W: Giant of Steam* (Boulder, Colorado: Pruett Publishing Company, 1980).

74 The nomenclature for describing steam locomotives used here, and throughout this book, is the Whyte system of classification, with the first number indicating leading wheels; the second, driving (powered) wheels; and the third, trailing wheels. When there are more than three numbers, the middle numbers denote different sets of powered driving wheels in articulated locomotives such as the N&W Class A and Class Y locomotives. For an explanation of the Whyte system, see B. A. Botkin and Alvin F. Harlow, eds., *A Treasury of Railroad Folklore* (New York: Crown Publishers, 1953), 467.

75 For a list of surviving Norfolk and Western steam locomotives, see http://www.nwhs.org/qna/SurvivingNWSteam.html.

76 Link and Hensley, *Steam, Steel & Stars*, 129–30.

77 Three other Class Ms are known to survive, all in Virginia. See http://www.nwhs.org/qna/SurvivingNWSteam.html.

78 By Lucius Beebe (New York: E. P. Dutton Company, 1947).

79 This author covered Hastings's role in creating environmental railroad photography extensively in "Artist of the Rail: Phil Hastings," *Railroad History* 198 (Spring–Summer 2008): 66–78. A look at Clegg's photography, without a focus on Beebe, awaits an author.

80 Rolling stock is a railroad term used to refer to wheeled assets: locomotives, passenger cars, freight cars, cabooses, and the like.

81 In its promotional materials, the Norfolk and Western Railway called its service area the "Land of Plenty." Since its tracks ran through Southside Virginia, Appalachia, and a part of the Ohio rustbelt, this name for the area can seem ironic today.

82 Garver, "Travelling Light," 91.

83 The railroad (N&W timetable and station) name for Whitetop, Virginia, was White Top, Virginia, and in this book we use the N&W spelling.

84 Several of the images in *In the "Land of Plenty"* echo the railroad-subject work of Walker Evans—compare plate 138 with Evans's *Company Houses Along Railroad Tracks. Scott's Run near Morgantown, West Virginia. Osage, West Virginia* (LC-USF342-000892-A), and consider Link's use of posters in the images of Nella (Husk), North Carolina, and in plates 135 and 149 (Evans was fascinated by posters, and often included them in his photographs). As already mentioned, Link's depiction of Jimbo, the "hound of Husk," also echoes a well-known Evans photograph that appeared in *Fortune* magazine in 1953, a couple of years before Link started his Norfolk and Western project. For easy access to Evans's FSA photographs, see the Library of Congress website.

85 According to the *O. Winston Link Negative Index* on file at the O. Winston Link Museum.

86 For more detail on Link's technical methods of photography, see *The Last Steam Railroad in America*, 37–42, and Jim Boyd, "Master of the Night," *Railfan* 1:8 (Fall 1976): 26–37. The list of Link's assistants is based on Tom Garver's unpublished synopsis, "O. Winston Link: Details of His Trips to the Norfolk and Western Railway" (April 2003; edited and with annotations added, May 2007). The seminal 1982 article by Allan Ripp, "Night Tricks," in *American Photographer* (June 1982): 42–53, contains a sidebar, page 52, with an excellent discussion of the inherent properties of flashbulbs and why they advantaged Link's work versus other lighting sources, such as stroboscopic flashguns.

87 See item 214 at http://www.loc.gov/rr/record/nrpb/registry/nrpb-master list.html.

From the late 1950s through the early 1980s, O. Winston Link was better known for his recordings of railroad sounds, five albums and one single, than he was for his photographs. While documenting the last days of the Norfolk and Western Railway in steam, Link produced a large archive of sound recordings. This CD features Link's sound recordings of the Norfolk and Western, most of them previously unreleased, that were selected both for their quality and for their connection to the text and photographs featured in this book.

The sound tracks below are presented in the same order as either the persons recorded, or the photographs taken simultaneously with them, appear in the text and plates. This allows the reader to experience the descriptions, images, and sounds as a multisensory experience. When the sound track is connected to a specific photograph in the book, the plate number and NW negative number are provided.

INTRODUCTION: THE END OF STEAM

Track 1

BEN DULANEY Winston Link and Norfolk and Western public relations manager Ben Bane Dulaney, whose role in Link's Norfolk and Western project is outlined in the introduction, chat during their trip behind Class J #611, on a passenger train just west of Salem, Virginia, in June 1958. Link received N&W's support in his effort to document the end of steam operations (see pages 17–18).

RAILROADERS

Track 2

NW 1161 (PLATE 6) A Norfolk and Western mechanic inspects the valve gear of a Class J during a station stop at Roanoke, Virginia. When struck with a hammer, defects in the rods that were difficult to see with the naked eye would make a unique sound. Photo NW 1161 shows him at work.

Track 3

NW 1118 (PLATE 34) Usher Buck Stewart announces the departure of Train #3, the *Pocahontas*, at the N&W passenger station in Roanoke, Virginia, in August 1956.

Track 4

NW 1858 (PLATE 38) The exhaust of a Class Y is deafening as it shoves the rear of a heavy coal train east, ascending Blue Ridge Grade, in June 1958. Photo NW 1858 depicts this operation from the view of the rear brakeman, who will uncouple the pusher from the caboose "on the fly" at the summit.

Track 5

NW 1977 (PLATE 42) An eastbound train whistles to announce its approach, and then stops to await a pusher to assist with the ascent of Blue Ridge Grade. At the same time, a Class Y, running light (a railroad term for a locomotive running without a train), passes westbound at Boaz Siding in Vinton, Virginia, in June 1958. Link photographed a night scene of a helper locomotive crew waiting for their next assignment at the "Honey Hole" at the same location.

Track 6

ON LOCOMOTIVES Winston Link and the crew of Y-6a #2160 chat while running light up Blue Ridge Grade, in June 1958. Link struggles to capture the volume of the whistle, using the gain setting on his recorder.

IRON HORSES

Track 7

NW 2182 (PLATE 55) The Second Pigeon Creek Shifter with Y-6b #2190 performs its work between Williamson and Kermit, West Virginia, in March 1960. After whistling for several road crossings, the train slows to a crawl. NW 2182 and NW 2186 (plate 14) are photos of the Second Pigeon Creek Shifter, taken during the same trip.

SIDE BY SIDE

Track 8

NW 123C (PLATE 76) As water drips off the walls, Class Y-6 #2136 with a train passes by inside Mingo Tunnel in Williamson, West Virginia, in March 1960. Link's synchronized flash in photo NW 123C captured the moment.

Track 9

NW 1350 (PLATE 79) A streamlined Class K with a passenger train rushes past with elaborate whistling, indicating a stop at the next station. Link was intrigued by the name of this isolated location along the Shenandoah Division: Solitude. He framed a streamlined Class K leading Train #2 within the sign at Solitude, Virginia, in photo NW 1350.

Track 10

NW 32K (PLATE 80) Class A #1224 and Class Y-6a #2160 pull a heavy coal train up Blue Ridge Grade, in June 1958. When two steam locomotives were used at the front of a train, the crew in the lead locomotive was respon-

sible for whistle communication. The engineer demonstrates his skill with the huge locomotive's whistle, playing it like a musical instrument. With the N&W's support, Link arranged the scene shown in *Highball for the Doubleheader* (NW 32K) to capture a similar train ascending the grade at Bonsack, Virginia, in 1959.

Track 11

NW 1998 (PLATE 83) The sound of the exhaust of a Class A ascending Blue Ridge Grade eastbound, in October 1957, is both loud and sharp. Photo NW 1998 records a similar occasion on a sweeping curve near the summit in Blue Ridge, Virginia.

Track 12

MRS. GRAY Winston Link chats with the crew of Y-6a #2160, running light up Blue Ridge Grade for its next assignment. While passing a nearby house, Link relates a story about Mrs. Gray, who lived there.

Track 13

NW 1851 (PLATE 93) The sound of the exhaust of a Class Y pusher working at full throttle on Blue Ridge Grade, in June 1958, is nearly a constant roar.

IN THE "LAND OF PLENTY"

Track 14

NW 704 (PLATE 108) In photo NW 704, Jack Hash and his son Dan watch Class Y-5 #2110 exit Montgomery Tunnel, near Christiansburg, Virginia, ascending Christiansburg Mountain.

Track 15

CLASS Y ON THE SHENANDOAH DIVISION A Class Y passes with its train, in spring 1956. Sounds like these were common to people living along the N&W Shenandoah Division. Link made photos in locations like Lithia and Vesuvius, Virginia, to illustrate the interaction of the railroad and area residents.

Track 16

NW 1136 (PLATE 118) Crossing bells give ample notice of an approaching Class Y-6–powered freight, in the summer of 1956. The train slows down as it passes Link's recorder. In NW 1136, a similar freight passes a grade crossing and the N&W station at Vesuvius, Virginia.

SELECTED, CHRONOLOGICAL BIBLIOGRAPHY

HOW IT WAS DONE

Track 17

NW 834 (PLATE 167) A Class Y pulling Train #51 switches at Shenandoah Junction, West Virginia, as heard on Link's first surviving recording, made in the summer of 1956. The improvements in recording technique that Link made following his early efforts are evident in the excellent recordings made just two years later. In photo NW 834, George Thom adjusts the equipment during an early recording session, in 1956.

Track 18

NW 1826 (PLATE 173) Link explains how he gets a close-up recording of the distinctive connecting-rod clank of a Class Y pusher running light on Blue Ridge Grade, in June 1958. Photo NW 1826 illustrates one of the recording sessions on a Class Y helper on Blue Ridge Grade.

Track 19

NW 2040 (PLATE 175) Link describes conditions in the baggage car, where he is recording Class J #602 pulling the eastbound *Cavalier* between Williamson and Matewan, West Virginia, in December 1958. Winston works with the Ampex recorder during the trip where photo NW 2040 was taken.

Track 20

KEYSTONE, WEST VIRGINIA Link describes the scene during a station stop in Keystone, West Virginia, on the westbound *Cavalier*, pulled by Class J #603, in January 1959.

Track 21

S-1 AND GP-9 SWITCHING AT ROANOKE STATION Illustrating the transition period between steam and diesel, a Class S 0-8-0 and an EMD GP-9 road-switcher carry out similar duties at the Roanoke, Virginia, passenger station, in August 1958. This is an example of the exceptional quality of the stereo recordings Winston Link made before steam operations ended on the Norfolk and Western.

Train #2 at Waynesboro, Virginia, January 21, 1955 (NW 1). *Trains* 15:10 (August 1955): 42. (First known appearance of a Link N&W series photo in print; also the first photo in the N&W series.)

"Flash Bulb Artist Photographs the Norfolk and Western: O. Winston Link, New York Photographer, Captures Fascinating Night-Time Scenes Along Our Railroad." *Norfolk and Western Magazine* (October 1956): 580–83. (Text attributed to Ben Bane Dulaney.)

"Photo Section . . . The Man Behind the Camera . . . O. Winston Link." *Trains* 17:5 (March 1957): 44.

"The Mixed Train." *Trains* 17:9 (July 1957): 31–43. (Text attributed to David P. Morgan.)

"Steam After Dark: Norfolk & Western at Night, Photographed by O. Winston Link." *Trains* 18:1 (November 1957): 30–43. (Text attributed to David P. Morgan.)

"Night Trick" on the Norfolk and Western Railway. (Roanoke, Virginia: Norfolk and Western Railway, 1957). (Text attributed to Ben Bane Dulaney.)

Highball for the Double Header, Blue Ridge Grade, East of Roanoke, Va., 1959 (160), *Luray Crossing, with Y-6 Locomotive and Freight, Luray, Va., 1956* (194), *Y-6 Locomotive on the Turntable, Shaffer's Crossing Yards, Roanoke, Va., 1955* (195), in Lucius Beebe and Charles Clegg, *Great Railroad Photographs, U.S.A.* (Berkeley, California: Howell-North Books, 1964), 160, 194, 195. (Believed to be the first book appearances of Link's Norfolk and Western photos.)

Boyd, Jim. "Master of the Night." *Railfan* 1:8 (Fall 1976): 26–37.

Ripp, Allan. "Night Tricks." *American Photographer* 8:6 (June 1982): 42–53.

Stephen, Andrew. "Closely Observed Trains." *Sunday* (London) *Times Magazine* (June 19, 1983): 30–38.

Ellis, Ainslie. "Egg Stove and Bananas." *The British Journal of Photography* (July 29, 1983): 781–86.

Grundberg, Andy. "Photography View: Documents of the Steam Train That Approach the Surreal." *The New York Times* (September 4, 1983): H20.

Martin, Rupert. *Night Trick by O. Winston Link: Photographs of the Norfolk & Western Railway, 1955–60* (exhibition catalog) (London: The Photographers' Gallery, 1983).

Ghost Trains: Railroad Photographs of the 1950s by O. Winston Link (exhibition catalog) (Norfolk, Virginia: The Chrysler Museum, 1983).

Machalabra, Daniel. "Fame Arrives Late for a Photographer of Trains at Night—O. Winston Link, 71, an Artist of the Late Steam Age, Is Acclaimed as a Virtuoso." *Wall Street Journal* (January 13, 1986; Eastern edition): 1.

Link, O. Winston, photographs; text by Tim Hensley, afterword by Thomas H. Garver. *Steam, Steel & Stars: America's Last Steam Railroad* (New York: Harry N. Abrams, Inc., 1987).

Yule, G. Paul, director. *O. Winston Link: Trains That Passed in the Night* (Berwick Universal Pictures, 1990). Color, 52 minutes. (Produced for Independent Television [ITV] in Great Britain and first presented October 1990.)

"Link, O. Winston." *Current Biography* 56:6 (June 1995): 361–65.

Liddell, Marlane A. "Steam Locomotives Steal the Spotlight." *Smithsonian* 26:7 (October 1995): 62–69.

Link, O. Winston, photographs; text by Thomas H. Garver. *The Last Steam Railroad in America* (New York: Harry N. Abrams, Inc., 1995).

Jones, Malcolm. "The Most Beautiful Trains in the World." *Preservation* 51:6 (November/December 1999): 30–36, 73.

Steam Locomotives of the 20th Century: O. Winston Link and Naotaka Hirota (exhibition catalog) (Hokuto, Japan: Kiyosato Museum of Photographic Arts, 2000).

Del Vecchio, Mike. "O. Winston Link, 1914–2001." *Railfan & Railroad* 20:5 (May 2001): 46–47.

Keefe, Kevin P. "Link: Where You'd Least Expect Him." *Trains* 61:6 (June 2001): 42–49.

Boyd, Jim. "The O. Winston Link Museum." *Railfan & Railroad* 22:10 (October 2003): 62.

Lyden, Anne M. *Railroad Vision: Photography, Travel, and Perception* (Los Angeles: The J. Paul Getty Museum, 2003).

Reevy, Tony. "Print & Image: O. Winston Link." *Railroad History* 190 (Spring–Summer 2004): 78–99.

Yule, Paul, director. *The Photographer, His Wife, Her Lover* (Berwick Universal Pictures, 2006). Color.

Garver, Thomas H. "O. Winston Link." *NRHS Bulletin* 73 (Summer 2008), 4–43.

Stone, Ted, director. *What a Picture I Got!* (O. Winston Link Museum, 2009). Color, 32 minutes (produced by WDBJ7, 2001).

Link, Albert, Jr. *O. Winston Link: A Family Album* (Mahopac, New York: TC Graphics, 2009).

Olaf Haensch, "Der verlorene Olymp" (20–33), Olaf Haensch, "Ein wahrer Frcund" (34–37), Olaf Haensch and Kim Parker, "Welcome to Roanoke, VA!" (38–43) and Olat Haensch, "Kohlerevier und Dampfbastion" (46–53), in "Magie der Nacht," *ModellEisenBahner* 12 (Spezial) (December 2010–March 2011).

ACKNOWLEDGMENTS

Tony Reevy: First, this book would not have been possible without the work of the O. Winston Link Museum's O. Winston Link Book Committee, led by Chair Tom Hoover and O. Winston Link Museum Director Kim Parker and also including Bill and Ellen Arnold, David Foster, and this author. Kim and the staff of the O. Winston Link Museum deserve thanks for their work on the project, above and beyond Kim's committee service. And, as usual, I find that friend, colleague, photographer, and writer Jeff Brouws has been there before me with regard to O. Winston Link and Link's photographic legacy; I thank Jeff for his ideas and comments. I would like to acknowledge the publication of my article on O. Winston Link, from which portions of *Life Along the Line: O. Winston Link's Photographs of the Norfolk & Western Railway, 1955–1960* were drawn, in *Railroad History* 190 (Spring–Summer 2004), pages 78–99. I also would like to thank then *Railroad History* editor Mark Reutter, and present editor Pete Hansen, as well as those interviewed for the article: Steve Barry, Kent Chrisman, Tom Garver, Ben Halpern, and Bill Johnson. I would also like to acknowledge the invitation from the O. Winston Link Museum to keynote the event honoring the fiftieth anniversary of the first O. Winston Link Norfolk and Western project photo, NW 1, in Waynesboro, Virginia, on January 21, 2005. I have used a portion of my keynote address in writing *Life Along the Line: O. Winston Link's Photographs of the Norfolk & Western Railway, 1955–1960*. Special thanks goes out to Tom Garver—who served as Link's assistant, helped advance his career in the art photography world, and then helped found scholarship focusing on O. Winston Link. He continues to foster efforts to advance our knowledge and understanding of Link's photographs. Thank you to my wife, Caroline Weaver, for reading and commenting on a draft of this manuscript. And, finally, thank you to my family—Caroline, Lindley, and Ian—for their patience (as Daddy monopolized the computer) and for their support. And thanks to Laura Dozier for her wonderful editing of this book, with thanks to her colleagues at Abrams as well.

The O. Winston Link Book Committee: The Committee would like to thank Conway Link, who owns the copyright to O. Winston Link's photographs, for permission to reproduce the images, and for his thoughtful afterword. We would also like to thank Dave Stephenson, whose vast knowledge of the O. Winston Link sound archive, and careful documentation of the archive, were essential in the effort to select sounds to accompany this book. Dave, the author of *O. Winston Link's N&W Recordings: More Sounds of Steam Railroading*, was generous in the time and effort he devoted to make this part of the project a success. We also thank Louis M. Newton, who worked in the N&W Mechanical Department during the years when O. Winston Link was capturing the last of N&W steam on film. Louis provided critical assistance with regard to N&W history, locations, and corporate terminology. The committee would also like to thank Committee member and O. Winston Link Museum Director Kim Parker, and the staff of the Museum; this project would not have been possible without their work. Finally, the committee would like to thank Scott Lothes for his wonderful foreword.

Tony Reevy, senior associate director of the Institute for the Environment at the University of North Carolina at Chapel Hill, is a graduate of North Carolina State University, UNC–Chapel Hill, and Miami University. He is a David P. Morgan Award winner (2006) and a Pushcart Prize nominee. His previous publications include poetry, nonfiction, and short fiction, including the nonfiction book *Ghost Train!*, and the poetry chapbooks *Green Cove Stop, Magdalena*, *Lightning in Wartime*, and *In Mountain Lion Country*. He resides in Durham, North Carolina, with his wife, Caroline Weaver, and their children, Lindley and Ian.

Scott Lothes (pronounced *lotus*) is executive director of the Center for Railroad Photography & Art (www.railphoto-art.org) in Madison, Wisconsin. He has a degree in mechanical engineering from Case Western Reserve University and spent three years as assistant editor of the engineering magazine *Sound & Vibration*. Lothes is a self-taught artist, and his photography and writing are widely published in *Trains, Railfan & Railroad*, and other railroad magazines, books, and websites. He grew up in southern West Virginia, not far from the locations of many of Link's night photographs along the Norfolk and Western.

Conway Link is the only child of O. Winston Link. He received a BS in mathematics and a BA in history from Louisiana Tech University, and an MA in mathematics from the University of Oklahoma, and did several years of graduate work in biostatistics and epidemiology. For thirty-four years he taught mathematics and statistics at Louisiana State University in Shreveport.

Link owns Gallery 1877 in Shreveport and is a partner in LouisianaLink LLC, which promotes his father's 1930s Louisiana images and later commercial work through exhibits and presentations. The preservation and rehabilitation of historic commercial buildings continues to be one of Link's top priorities.

The O. Winston Link Museum

The Collection of the O. Winston Link Museum is certainly focused on the Norfolk and Western project. Link captured the last days of steam operation on the N&W Railway in the late 1950s, but within the walls of these galleries, our visitors experience much more than just photographs. This collection is more than trains and rail operations. The images created by Link are vignettes into history and sociology. They are art; they are a part of the history of photography and they are a tool to share an era with every person. The Norfolk and Western project is the basis of the museum, but as viewers travel through our seven galleries, each area brings new knowledge and different perceptions. Our galleries are designed to showcase a complete awareness of the time period and the context in which Winston worked.

Editor: Laura Dozier
Designer: Darilyn Lowe Carnes
Production Manager: Anet Sirna-Bruder with Ankur Ghosh

Cataloging-in-Publication Data has been applied for and may be obtained from the Library of Congress.

ISBN: 978-1-4197-0372-0

Printed and bound in Hong Kong
10 9 8 7 6 5 4 3 2

Abrams books are available at special discounts when purchased in quantity for premiums and promotions as well as fundraising or educational use. Special editions can also be created to specification. For details, contact specialsales@abramsbooks.com or the address below.

ABRAMS
THE ART OF BOOKS SINCE 1949
115 West 18th Street
New York, NY 10011
www.abramsbooks.com

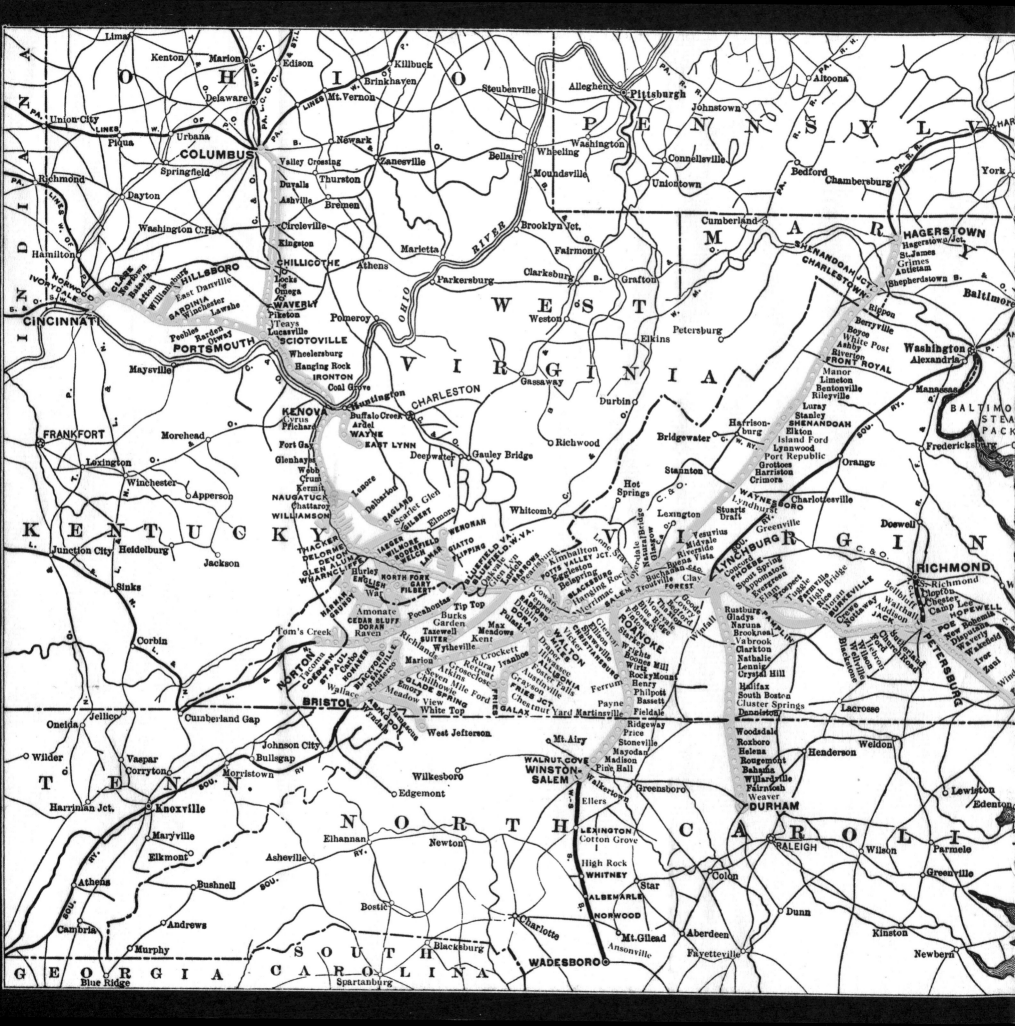